GOING GREEN USING DIATOMACEOUS EARTH HOW-TO TIPS

GOING GREEN USING DIATOMACEOUS EARTH HOW-TO TIPS

An Easy Guide Book Using A Safer Alternative, Natural Silica Mineral, Food Grade Insecticide: Tui Rose's Smart, Simple, & Safe Solutions Genie Series

For Homes, Gardens, Animals, Birds, Grains, Farms, Crops, Orchards, Buildings, & Environment:

Tui Rose R.N

Also author of:

* 1001 Green, Thrifty & Safer Home Solutions
* 501 Green, Thrifty & Safer Gardening Tips
* 501 Cat Chat & Dog Pow-Wow Pet Care Tips

Coming Soon

www.TuiRoseTips.com

Outskirts Press, Inc.
Denver, Colorado

Edited by: Karen Stephenson, Quebec, Canada
Cover design by: Dean Nixon Design www.deannixondesign.com

Outskirts Press, Inc.
http://www.outskirtspress.com

ISBN: 978-1-4327-4443-4

Library of Congress Control Number: 2009907721

Includes Table of Contents, Bibliographical References, and Index

Outskirts Press and the "OP" logo are trademarks belonging to Outskirts Press, Inc.

PRINTED IN THE UNITED STATES OF AMERICA

Endorsement

Tui Rose has certainly come up with a novel approach to the topic of Diatomaceous Earth. I am impressed. Quite an interesting and admirable undertaking. A lot of what she writes is new to me.

—Richard Breese, Geologist

Acknowledgments

The majority of the information incorporated in this book is from fact based data and reference sources—however, there are some people I must thank for their support, help and guidance.

Special gratitude to Richard O.Y. Breese (geologist) and expert on Diatomaceous Earth for his helpful comments on the aspects of geology and mineralogy for this book.

Gratitude to Dick Evons, an expert in the field of Diatomaceous Earth. He has contributed to my research on Diatomaceous Earth (DE) including some of the information on Food Codex DE, the cautions and hazards of additives, inert ingredients, crystalline silica industrial grade DE, governing requirements, standards, and product labeling issues regarding DE.

In a category unique unto itself, I must acknowledge the passion and enthusiasm of Wally Tharp. In the early days of my research into DE for another book I was writing many years ago, his enthusiasm and passion further spurred my awareness of this amazing mineral and to seek answers to the wide variety of claims made about it. Wally Tharp was an early advocate, promoting his ideas for its use, starting in the 1960's. For this he will always have my personal thanks.

Although the identity of contributors to the Anecdotal Success Stories in Chapter's Two through Five is kept confidential to protect their privacy, these results and experiences are very much appreciated to expand our ideas. By highlighting other users' experiences, their ideas show us how we can quite easily transition from using poisons to this natural product, thereby making the quality of our lives safer and healthier. We can learn from them how to control insect challenges inside our buildings, on our pets, gardens, farms, playgrounds, and even on large acreage without resorting to the use of toxic chemicals.

Special thanks to Steve Tvedten, who shared some of the news articles, information and facts in Chapter Seven regarding the detrimental effects of toxic chemical pesticides and governing or associated agencies.

Thank you to editor Karen Stephenson, Canada for her work and keen interest in this subject; to my son Dean Nixon for his generosity, artistic talent, cover design and support; and to my daughter Shyama for her loving support.

Disclaimer

This book is intended as an educational reference volume only, to help readers further their own investigations in order to make informed decisions. The author, editor, endorsers, sponsors, partners and publisher hold no responsibility for any detrimental effects whatsoever resulting from the use of Diatomaceous Earth (DE), or the brand or quality of DE chosen by the user. The responsibility rests solely with the discretion of the user. The author is not responsible for any omissions, errors, or misunderstandings about DE. Laws surrounding this substance may change at any time and may need to be updated in future editions.

Although the author has used DE for over a decade she has not personally tried or tested all the methods, brands, and uses for DE mentioned within this book. This information is a comprehensive smorgasbord of reports and research materials from various scientific, federal, health, and independent news and journal sources, coupled with handy comments from a few competitive experts—those considered "old-hands" with 20 to 40 years of individual experience in this field of DE usage. Additionally, interesting contributions are matched with various chapters; ideas and tips that were obtained from over 50 actual DE users—their down-to-earth anecdotal experiences, endorsements, and testimonials collected from a broad cross-section of rural and urban applications. Many of these users have long become experts themselves—some for decades. Their names have been changed or omitted to protect their privacy. Although they share their own personal experiences and successes on a variety of uses and applications for DE, the reader's results may not necessarily be the same. To the best of the author's knowledge, these anecdotal sources and statements are credible and accurate.

Any references to commercial products or trade names are made with the understanding that no discrimination is intended and no endorsement by the publisher, author, editor or sponsors is implied. There are many manufacturers with varying opinions, printed documents, qualities of mine deposits, and mining, manufacturing and production methods.

The author recommends using only food grade DE. Wherever food grade DE is referenced in this book, it's written with the assumption that the consumer has taken the responsibility upon themselves to be prudent and thoroughly research the brand they buy and use, and to make sure it meets the FDA's food grade or Food Codex criteria, and the GRAS (Generally Recognized as Safe) standards. To check on the quality of DE, the consumer needs to deal directly with the manufacturer, their representative or distributor, and ask to view their Material Safety Data Sheet (MSDS).

Users of any DE product should carefully read and follow all label and packaging instructions when using Anti-Caking agent, Inert Carrier, Grain Storage Protectant, or various brands of DE insecticides, and not rely solely on the suggestions in this book.

The DE referred to in this book is not a toxic chemical, but a naturally occurring silicon dioxide mineral (sometimes referred to as silica) in processed powder form, which can be mixed with water and applied with various types of spray applicators at the discretion of the user. Each person can explore the many options provided, and determine what works best for their own specific needs.

The author recommends that anyone wishing to treat animals or birds for internal parasites should seek professional advice from a veterinarian who is familiar with the use of DE, or a researcher or qualified technician in this field, such as a County Extension Agent.

It is strongly advised that any reader or consumer wishing to ingest food grade DE as an anti-parasitic, intestinal cleanser and detoxifier, or nutritional supplement should check with the company who manufacturers DE for ingestion such as a Trace Mineral Supplement for quality and directions. The consumer should also seek the advice of a medical or nutritional professional who is a skilled and knowledgeable practitioner in this field. The author is not into business of providing personal consultation.

Opinions vary, but as the reader's knowledge base and practical experience broadens, one will be able to make their own informed decisions and draw their own conclusions about this amazing ancient substance that comes from Mother Nature.

Table of Contents

CHAPTER FIVE
Application Tools & Methods For Using
Diatomaceous Earth (DE)..75

CHAPTER SIX
Diatomaceous Earth (DE) Benefits In Products

CHAPTER SEVEN
Health Risks Linked To Toxic Pesticides

CHAPTER EIGHT
Safety Precautions For Diatomaceous Earth (DE).......119

Introduction

Why do we need a book on Diatomaceous Earth (DE)? As a natural alternative to toxic chemicals, there simply wasn't a single book available on this topic until now, albeit a guidebook that offers both background information and practical tips to help a wide variety of consumers find a way to be safer in their own skin and environment. Unfortunately, due to the lack of information, millions of people have either used dangerous chemicals or been exposed to them (often unknowingly)—all with uncertain consequences. Despite DE having existed as a natural resource for hundreds of centuries, toxic insecticides have reigned over the pesticide industry for more than a half-century with their products dominating retail shelves, homes, and literally everywhere, amounting to billions of dollars a year in sales for the chemical manufacturers. It's interesting to note—more than $1 billion per year is spent on fleas and ticks alone, yet people still complain these products do not always work effectively due to the insects' ability to develop resistance to such poisons.

As a concerned mother and registered nurse of thirty five years, Tui set out in 1993 to do her own research to find some safer solutions as she was writing another book on natural remedies for the home and garden at that particular time. When she came upon Diatomaceous

Earth, of which she had never heard before, she wondered why this could have escaped her knowledge for so long.

Searching for literature on Diatomaceous Earth, she found only obscure and heavily encumbered university science books existed. Even then, they had a narrow focus, mainly upon the geological and chemical background of the original source of DE as a sedimentary mineral rock. Further, these intellectual books do not provide for everyday practical utilization and education of the average consumer, or for the health practitioner who needs to expand their knowledge for counseling in the "green" arena. These days, patients are becoming more and more demanding of their practitioners to help them come up with safer and greener alternatives which they can easily obtain, and also know how to use to keep themselves and their families healthy.

So, Tui saw the need to fill the literature void and she ambitiously undertook to write a book on Diatomaceous Earth. During her time of research, Tui began using DE herself. Friends, neighbors and family would often make the same comment, "It's great you found a safer alternative to chemicals, but what is it? How do you use it? How does it work?" Tui literally had to do the research for herself. She came across some experts in the field of DE, a few of whom had some forty years of experience in the field of DE mining, manufacturing or usage. Documenting their knowledge imparted to her, she combined that with research data from governing agencies, and health, scientific and education journals and organizations. After some 15 years, Tui finally strung it all together as a book with the goal of bridging the information gap with background history, and useful healthful how-to tips to help the reader and consumer know what it's all about, why they should use it, and what to do with it in their effort to make greener choices in creating their own safer place.

Who can use this book? This practical guide for using Diatomaceous Earth (DE) is not only for consumers but also for health practitioners who prefer to guide their clients to focus on natural least-toxic alternatives to chemical pesticides. These how-to tips benefit a broad cross-section of the community: the unborn fetus, children, pregnant and lactating women, home owners, gardeners, pet owners, bird keepers, animal breeders, boarding kennel operators, veterinarians, and farmers. DE is used to benefit dogs, cats, cows, horses, alpachas, goats, pigs, sheep, poultry and ostriches. It is also used on crops, orchards, public play-grounds and parks; in harvesting, milling, packing, storing, and transporting facilities for nuts, grains, seeds, and legumes; and by pest control operators (PCOs) for safer use in places such as schools, city and county facilities, sewers, medical establishments, retirement and convalescent homes, food handling facilities and warehouses, hotels, and agricultural fair grounds.

Incidentally, most toxic chemical insecticides have never been tested by the Environmental Protection Agency (EPA) before being released onto the market. Further, hundreds more continue to be removed only after years of proving to be harmful or deadly. Meanwhile, hundreds of other new poisonous insecticides are continually being introduced to retail shelves. There's almost no place left on earth that has not been exposed, and not one of us will develop immunity to all these chemicals.

It's time for change! But what needs to change? Firstly, awareness of the potentially perilous situation we have gotten ourselves into by using chemical pesticides. This book explains the many proven health risks linked to toxic chemical pesticides, while putting alternative practical tools at your fingertips to make safer changes in your own space at least.

More public demand needs to become a reality before an abundance of easily available safer pesticide alternatives such as Diatomaceous Earth arrive on the mainstream market to stay. But, before the current situation can change at specific levels of governing regulations, manufacturing, and marketing, it seems consumers need to be further educated in order to be motivated enough to help facilitate the changes needed. So here's something sort of mind-boggling to think about and chew on—parts of this Introduction and Chapters Seven and Eight reveal serious areas of concern of which the author discovered are major roadblocks ahead begging to be removed, and which for so long have been thwarting the abundance of product and easy access to this safer solution to poisonous insecticides, which result in chemical borne diseases and disabilities still being discovered. Make no mistake, these chemicals and hormones can affect our health, and they can also change the genetic blue print of our loved ones and future generations. Let's face it, this issue is literally very close to home—our own homes. Your home! Your personal self!

While Diatomaceous Earth is not a panacea for all problems that bug us, its effectiveness and potential as a major alternative to solve most of our bug problems is much underestimated. Diatomaceous Earth is not simply an alternative; it's a preventative approach to all the health threats, ailments and suffering caused by toxic chemical pesticides. DE is as old as the dinosaurs—even used by ancient cultures in China, Greece and Egypt to preserve grain, seeds, nuts and legumes from disintegration by moisture, mold and insects. As long as DE is kept dry and remains undisturbed in the place of application it can last indefinitely, and be effective in some situations with a single application. But, where has DE been since its use in ancient cultures?

Unfortunately, like many ancient things, Diatomaceous Earth's benefits have been largely forgotten, replaced or substituted by new, so-called "improved" technologies of the chemical pesticide industry in the last sixty years. While the chemical industry has produced many beneficial products, it has also been the source of harmful environmental and health consequences. Now with the results of medical research as seen in some of the news articles in Chapter Seven, Diatomaceous Earth is making a comeback due to popular consumer demand.

The next part of this Introduction briefly summarizes each chapter, highlighting information about Diatomaceous Earth pertaining to the different and specific target areas, benefits, practical tips, recipes, application methods, tools, anecdotal evidence (examples of how others used DE and their successes), precautions, and the health risks of toxic chemical insecticides.

Chapter One: What On Earth Is Diatomaceous Earth (DE) And How Does It Work? DE is composed of the skeletal remains of millions of fossilized microscopic diatoms that once flourished as a form of golden brown aquatic algae or plankton that lived in ocean and lake waters as a food source for all kinds of aquatic creatures. From as far back as the beginning of the Cenozoic Era some 65 million years ago, diatoms have existed and contributed to the buildup of sediment on the ocean floor. Fossilizing over eons of time into soft powdery rock many feet thick, geological forces pushed these deposits up to the Earth's surface. Today, the deposits that are mined and milled into a whitish powder are primarily from diatoms that lived in lakes which evolved mostly in the Miocene Epoch or younger time periods roughly 25 million years ago.

The fossilized remains of these microscopic diatoms have remarkable and safe bug killing qualities when mined and milled to a fine powder. Diatomaceous Earth kills bugs by sticking to their waxy protective outer layer causing dehydration (chemical-like action) by absorbing their fluids, or possibly causing abrasion with subsequent loss of body fluids, or interfering with their breathing mechanism and mobility by mechanical action. DE also has a deterring factor that acts to fence bugs out, without the undesirable chemical effects, and eventual resistance that occurs with poisons, which creates super bugs.

As long as a bug comes into physical contact with the powder they will eventually succumb. Some bugs like carpenter ants die almost instantly, while other types of bugs with harder exoskeletons may take a few hours, or a day or two. But, patience is well worth the health and safety benefits. This ancient substance is truly a modern day natural treasure—a safer and simple solution to our everyday insecticidal needs of eliminating bugs.

Chapter Two: Diatomaceous Earth (DE) Uses As A Safer Home And Garden Insecticide: Food grade Diatomaceous Earth can be safely used in the home and garden around children and pets. Dozens of "how-to" tips are provided for natural ways to treat an A-Z list of bugs through the dehydrating powers of Diatomaceous Earth without chemical nerve poisons. Several anecdotal success stories by other users help to expand individual ideas and ways to use Diatomaceous Earth around the home and garden.

Diatomaceous Earth also has a number of other helpful novelty uses not widely known. Food grade Diatomaceous Earth is safe to use like baking soda to deodorize kitty litter, shoes, refrigerators, vacuum cleaner bags and garbage cans. It can soak up motor oil, (even contain large industrial oil spills), soothe bug bites and bee stings, kill fleas, ticks and lice, resist mold and moisture, retard tarnishing when stored with silver, act as a gentle metal polisher and a soft scrub when slightly moistened, and preserve leaves and flowers for dried arrangements. It is hard to imagine any other natural or synthetic substance that comes close to accomplishing so many solutions to so many challenges, and for so many different kinds of people and uses.

Chapter Three: Diatomaceous Earth (DE) For Use In Grain Storage For Humans And Animals: Diatomaceous Earth *Grain Storage Protectant* is used for preserving grains, nuts, seeds, legumes, rice and more, for both animal and human use from damage by many insects including grain weevils and their larvae. Pure Diatomaceous Earth with no additives, being a natural desiccant, also helps to prevent grains from destruction by moisture and mold. Many recipes are offered for ways to preserve quart jars of whole grains in the pantry, to 25-pound bags, and 100-pound to 1-ton storage containers. There are even recipes for how to protect entire food cellars, grain storage warehouses, farms and mills. A few anecdotal success stories are provided for grain storage.

Chapter Four: Diatomaceous Earth (DE) For Agricultural Uses: Diatomaceous Earth for animals comes under the label *Anti-Caking Agent, Grain Protectant,* or *Inert Carrier* and has been used for decades in agriculture both externally and internally as a *feed additive,* and in horticulture. *Anti-caking agent* is just what it says; it's a material that is added to another powder, animal feed or grain to facilitate better handling and mixability by keeping it clump-free and consequently free-flowing when poured. It has a beneficial effect on health not only when applied externally to animals and birds but also when added to their feed by providing natural trace minerals for growth and strength, among many other benefits.

The many anecdotal success stories from farmers attribute Diatomaceous Earth to making sick and skinny animals well again: eliminating scours and intestinal and external parasites; keeping coats and eyes shiny; reducing veterinarian bills; increasing milk production; and keeping animals generally more contented. The manure of animals fed Diatomaceous Earth has reduced odor, which keeps farmers, animals and birds happy due to the reduction of flies. Diatomaceous Earth can be safely used in poultry houses and even on the chickens and also on other birds such as ostriches. It can be spread over manure around the barn, stable, poultry house or milking parlor. It can be applied on top of and around feed-bags and bins to prevent damage by grain insects, and it can be applied on crops and orchards right up to the time of harvest. Anecdotal success stories are provided for ideas on how to apply Diatomaceous Earth to birds and animals, on farms and large commercial scale acreage of crops and orchards.

Chapter Five: Application Tools & Methods To Get The Best Results From Using Diatomaceous Earth (DE): This section provides practical methods, tips and solutions for applying Diatomaceous Earth in almost any situation, no matter how small or large the challenge by using a variety of applicators: hose-end sprayers for applying a liquid solution, pest pistols, accordion puffers, back-packs and tractor sprays—even airplanes. Electrostatic ionizers, when attached to these applicators use magnetic polarity to make the Diatomaceous Earth stick better to the underside of leaves, tree canopies and to reach dense foliage, or to efficiently and effectively cover and treat very large areas.

Chapter Six: Diatomaceous Earth (DE) Benefits For Human Ingestion: Although not approved by the Food and Drug Administration (FDA) for human ingestion in the USA, *food grade* Diatomaceous Earth has been used for decades in capsules or powder form for human ingestion especially in Europe and Asia as an anti-parasitic, intestinal detoxifier and Trace Mineral Supplement. Dosages are included as anecdotal suggestions by other practitioners or users.

Chapter Seven: Alarming Health Risks Linked To Toxic Chemical Pesticides & Why Diatomaceous Earth (DE) Is Better For Health: Over 90 percent of American households use toxic chemical pesticides and household products. However, due to rising public awareness, blind faith in routine pesticide treatments and exposure, once mistakenly considered the norm, have been proven to be not healthy or acceptable.

Alarmed consumers have become more educated about the unhealthy consequences of absorbing these toxins through the skin, inhalation, or ingestion. Exposure can easily come through contamination of carpets, floors, pet bedding, and clothing; and playing, eating or sleeping facilities; as well as our food and water supply. Consumers are gradually developing a healthier attitude, a new surge of interest, and a steadily increasing demand for safer and non-toxic alternative solutions to replace harmful insecticides.

This section contains summaries of over thirty medical and scientific articles related to the health risks of toxic chemical pesticides. Toxic chemicals are non-selective, with the ability to kill friend and foe alike. Alarm bells have sounded for decades, warning that everyone including our children and pets are increasingly over-exposed to an accumulation of disease-causing toxic insecticides. Chemical body-burden tests reveal that almost all of us have not one, but dozens of different chemicals in our blood stream.

Chemical pesticides can even be found in the most sacred of mother's milk, the unborn fetus, the newborn, and in most children affecting our genetic heritage. Since toxic pesticides have proven to cause millions of deaths, and a long list of damaging health effects, the Environmental Protection Agency (EPA) has been forced to remove many of these chemicals from the market, which they once approved, or they now impose substantial restrictions on other chemicals, most of which still have harmful effects.

DID YOU KNOW? Cancer strikes nearly one in every two men, and one in every three women today? Dr. Samuel Epstein, M.D., Professor Emeritus of Environmental Medicine at the University Of Illinois School Of Public Health, who is also chairman of the Cancer Prevention Coalition, reveals a startling upward spiraling trend in the incidence of major diseases especially cancer. He is particularly concerned about the risky use of toxic chemical cleaners and pesticides applied in our homes and gardens and rules out smoking or genetics as the cause of the increase to epidemic proportions over recent decades.

Are we sacrificing our long term health for the instant gratification of a quick toxic chemical fix and a few dead bugs? It's hard to ignore increases in the following types of cancer over the last few decades that were revealed by Dr. Epstein.

- Childhood cancers increased 40-50 percent.
- Breast cancer increased 60 to 65 percent.
- Testicular cancer (ages 28-35) increased 300 percent.
- Non-Hodgkin's lymphoma increased 100 percent.
- Brain cancer increased 80 to 90 percent.

- Dogs have a five times greater risk of getting canine lymphoma if they wear collars containing carcinogenic chemicals.

A one-time exposure to a toxic chemical insecticide has been proven to cause many life threatening ailments or diseases such as seizures, birth defects, childhood physical or mental developmental delays and disabilities, leukemia, lymphoma and other cancers. Aside from genetic damage, it can also cause a lifetime of any one of dozens of chronic diseases such as: asthma (the leading childhood disease), skin disorders, nervous system diseases such as ADHD, panic attacks, Parkinson's, and endocrine and reproductive disorders to name just a few.

While the author was gathering her research, an advocate and activist for safer alternatives told her his personal tragic story. Steve Tvedten used to be a chemical pest control operator until he and his family were stricken and disabled with an accumulation of toxic poisoning. Steve's son and uncle died, and he almost lost his own life. The man with a high IQ could not even count simple change and stop himself from shaking due to the damaging effects on his nervous system. When Steve recovered after a long struggle, he changed sides and became an advocate, manufacturer and activist for safer alternatives and a healthier environment. The result of such damage is billions of dollars in annual health care costs and personal suffering. Alternatively, food grade Diatomaceous Earth in the absence of chemical insecticides can provide a resolution to this ever-growing problem of health and safety issues.

Let's clear up a few misconceptions. Unfortunately, with chemicals, the inherent danger in how it can affect our health in the future is not easily seen coming. Further, the accumulative damage is not always acutely felt or known at the time—often not for years or even decades after exposure. Whereas Diatomaceous Earth is a visible whitish powder, chemicals are usually invisible once applied. The biggest mistake made is to believe chemical insecticides are not damaging or deadly if they cannot be visibly seen, and they must be safe if sold in our grocery stores. Another mistake we make is thinking a little bit won't hurt, or any contact now won't be detrimental later. Unfortunately, this kind of popular thinking has been proven by statistics to be either disastrous or deadly as the World Health Organization and Center for Disease Control has cautioned us about.

Chapter Eight: Safety Precautions For Diatomaceous Earth (DE): It's very important to note there are two principle forms of DE. Readers and consumers are cautioned—not all DE is *food grade* just because it comes from the earth. There is a vast difference between the quality of *food grade* DE *and industrial grade* DE to be aware of in order to choose the right kind of DE for the right job.

The only type of DE recommended in this book is natural-milled, unheated, *amorphous (non crystalline or non-calcined)* silicon dioxide, which is also referred to in the industry as food grade Diatomaceous Earth.

Industrial grade, (the one to be wary of) is unsafe for purposes described in this book and should not be used as an insecticide in the home, or in grains, or around birds and animals. Industrial grade DE is processed by heating at high temperatures, and is known as calcined or flux calcined DE, which creates harmful crystals. This *crystalline silica* is used primarily in commercial products for a variety of applications, such as in swimming pool and aquarium filters, road and construction materials, and some 1,500 other uses.

You may find yourself asking the same baffling question as the author did at one time: "Well, if DE is so good, then why hasn't it been used everywhere instead of poisons? If it's been around so long and it works, how did toxic chemical insecticides get a giant foothold in all our grocery stores, superstores, pharmacies and consequently in our homes?" New light is thrown on why this truly natural treasure has remained relatively in the dark and a mystery to the majority of the population for far too long.

This chapter discusses problems with official *red tape* and labeling issues, which need to be addressed and fixed in order to help both the sellers of Diatomaceous Earth use more appropriate and accurate verbiage on labels, and also to help consumers avoid any misunderstanding, misconceptions and confusion found on the labels.

Governing agencies have yet to resolve the many anomalies uncovered in this book regarding official laws that involve the Environmental Protection Agency (EPA), Food and Drug Administration (FDA), State labeling practices and registration of Diatomaceous Earth which literally has had a chokehold on the market for decades. For example, a pure food grade DE product used as an additive for animal feed, must require a hazardous warning on the label if the intended usage changes to a *pesticide*. Also, on a DE insecticide label it is illegal to use defining words such as: safe, safer, food grade, organic, natural, pure, non-toxic, least-toxic or healthier.

Then, how on earth can an ordinary person, or even a doctor for that matter, make a wise choice and determine if the pure food grade Diatomaceous Earth substance is non-toxic or a poison—especially when the label must provide the cautionary hazardous statement? There are no clues allowed on the label to project confidence to the buyer that they are choosing a safer product.

Unfortunately, changes needed at the government level in the EPA and State requirements are less likely to happen unless there is a much bigger public demand, or God forbid, some major attention-getting health crisis over chemicals.

Not only has there been a chokehold on product availability in major retail stores, there has also been a chokehold on information. Despite the fact Diatomaceous Earth has been available to consumers for about 70 years, most people including the medical profession, still know little or nothing about DE as an alternative, nor do they know what to do with it. Such a red tape road block against going green in recent decades has caused a national collective preference for poisons, along with an ignorance, and shortage of this safer solution. Amazingly, this miracle product is grown in Mother Nature's backyard and has existed for millions of years.

Unlike defensive driving where we consciously take the responsibility for our health and safety into our own hands, like buckling ourselves in and carefully putting our children into approved and properly installed car seats, most of the population does not protect themselves or their children from chemical hazards in the home with the same amount of care. Chemical poisons are often sprayed indiscriminately in kitchens where food is prepared, in bedrooms where we sleep, on furniture where we lounge, on carpets, or in the yard where children and pets play. We have created a train wreck waiting to happen to our beloved one's health. Unfortunately, for millions of victims of chemical insecticidal poisoning, it is too late to say, "if only we knew then, what we know now."

Incredibly, after so much damage has been done as a result of toxic chemical pesticides (that were once approved by trusted governing agencies), New York may be beginning to make a change to phase out the state's use of many pesticides. The website Environmental-expert.com issued a press release by Bergeson & Campbell, P.C on June 17, 2009, saying that the New York State Assembly on May 5, 2009, approved a measure to ban the use of most pesticides by state agencies and to establish an umbrella committee to manage the use of pesticides by the state. Pesticide use would be curtailed over a three year period, beginning in 2010 with those pesticides classed in Toxicity Category I by Environmental Protection Agency (EPA), followed by Category II pesticides in 2011, and remaining pesticides in 2012. Interestingly, this follows in the wake of many Canadian communities such as in Halibut and Quebec that have banned the use of pesticides more than a decade ago! Some smart environment and health conscious decision makers obviously do not trust their reliance upon the (EPA) and must know something the government doesn't to accept the responsibility of taking these drastic measures for eliminating risks to their citizens. Such actions will be rewarded with lowered healthcare costs.

Fortunately, in the last decade, there has been a surge of new public interest in Diatomaceous Earth. Over 40 years ago, Rachel Carson, a biologist wrote the popular book *Silent Spring* (from which a movie of the same name was made). She was one of the first activists to bring the dangers of chemical pesticides into the public limelight. It has taken us awhile, but with hindsight, we are now becoming more aware thanks to Rachel Carson and others who have followed suit, advocating for eliminating poisonous chemicals and replacing them with natural alternatives that promote good health.

A Google search of the phrase "natural home" yields over a half billion results. It's clear that a vast number of consumers are now interested in safer alternatives. There is no time like the present to discover, or rather rediscover Diatomaceous Earth while the need is growing. With city mayors in a race for "going green" these past few years, this book comes none too soon. BUT, we cannot go "green" as long as we are still reliant on health-damaging toxic pesticides that leave residues of destructive chemicals in our bodies, around our homes, gardens, schools, playgrounds, parks and buildings for dozens of years after just one application.

There are precautions of course, even for natural products, in which education is crucial for proper usage that are elucidated in this book. Still, it hardly seems an excuse for providing a dominance of poisons to the consumer market and creating a scarcity of safer solutions such as Diatomaceous Earth. If the trend continues and chemicals are allowed to stay, considering their multi-damaging affects to health as seen in Chapter Seven, shouldn't the chemical industry and the marketers of poisons be compensating consumers for the healthcare costs they need as a result of pesticide use?

The much needed change cannot be fully realized unless precious resources such as Diatomaceous Earth are unearthed, (unleashed from the red tape), to be made more easily available to main stream markets such as Walmarts, Walgreen, Target, CVS and Rite Aid pharmacies, Costco, Sams, Home Depot and other similar retailers. It is time now for all these chain and superstore administrators, buyers and managers to take the responsibility and depart from projecting a predominance of poisons onto customers—instead be proud to advertize and offer safer effective alternatives. All the above, are examples of places where toxic chemical pesticide poisons are liberally marketed with very little or zero competition from natural alternatives such as DE. When will these superstores and other supermarkets realize the power of their participation with their mayors and the society in "going green" by including this natural remedy on the *front* of their insecticide display shelves?

To help their market improve upon today's comparatively low demands and sales for safer non-toxic alternatives, these marketers and their wholesalers and distributors also need to get involved in demanding a change in the EPA laws. They should request a change to allow for the use of "safe" verbiage to help their customers make a wise choice when reading labels. Currently, there is much confusion over whether a non-toxic insecticide is a poison, or whether a poison is safe. Customers should not have to second guess and risk buying a poison because they cannot tell the difference, especially when the safer alternative label must give unnecessary hazardous cautions, other than a normal dust nuisance warning. The prime concern for these marketers is the power of their partnership with their customers in helping to keep us safe—to aid in protecting the areas for which we shop, which is where it matters most—right where we live, work, sleep and play, to benefit our health and those dearest to us.

As safer alternatives become more in demand, commercially available, and popularly recognized, these manufactures, distributors and retailers will find literally dozens of useful tips in this book about Diatomaceous Earth's applications and benefits to help their customers. This practical learning guide provides the long-awaited information for the seller, the consumer, and the health advocate.

Indeed, food grade Diatomaceous Earth fits the job description for choice and change to a safer natural pesticide—an amazing gift from Mother Nature.

1

What On Earth Is
Diatomaceous Earth (DE)?

An Ancient Treasure With Modern Heath Benefits

Diatomaceous Earth (DE) comes naturally from Mother Earth. It originated as a soft chalky, ancient rock called diatomite that was formed in sedimentary layers on the bottom of certain lakes and oceans over a span of millions of years. This rock is quarried from the bottom of dried up lake beds, some of which has been under the ocean since the Miocene Epoch. Diatomite deposits that are open-mined today are generally 25 million years or less in age.

Once the rock has been ground to an off-white powder, it is used for some 1,500 different uses in manufacturing, agriculture and horticulture. For the purposes of this book, DE is primarily used as a safer alternative insecticide and other uses as explained in the following chapters.

The diatomite rocky sediment has an interesting history of how it was formed. It is composed chiefly of uncountable billions of fossilized diatoms from which the name diatomaceous is derived. Diatoms are the skeletal remains of one-celled golden brown algae belonging to the Bacillariophyceae species that lived and flourished millions of years ago.

During each diatom's lifetime, an opalescent lattice-work of pores, rather like a honeycomb was formed within the plant's cell wall. This intricate structure absorbed silica from the water in which it lived. One of the ultimate sources of silica was volcanic ash from eruptions which partially dissolved after falling into the water. Hence Diatomaceous Earth is an opalescent major mineral consisting primarily of the element silicon dioxide (sometimes called silica) and about 14 trace minerals.

During its lifetime, the diatom's lattice structure was covered in a jelly secreted by the algae which contained cells for the purpose of photosynthesis. While providing up to 80 percent of our oxygen, these diatoms fed all kinds of aquatic creatures up and down the food chain. Protozoa, small fish, seals and whales all grazed on the pastures of algae diatoms, rich in soluble minerals, proteins and vitamins, which is why algae or plankton diatoms have been affectionately called *the meadow grass of the sea.*

Surviving widespread predation as fish fodder is no big deal to the prolific diatom since they can each divide in half every 4 to 36 hours, increasing their numbers at the phenomenal rate of about a billion in just two weeks. The diatom dies after a short but very prolific and useful life, some only living about 6 days. Once the plankton diatom is dead, only the silica rich lattice-like form remains after drifting to the sea floor or lake bed. Countless dead diatoms continually fall and pile upon the ocean or lake bottom. Together they fossilize over eons of time into sedimentary layers that accumulate slowly at the rate of about one foot every 20,000 years. Deposits of diatomite rock have been found to be anywhere from a few feet thick to surprisingly, hundreds or even thousands of feet deep.

The diatomite rock was pushed up towards the earth's surface from the bottom of the ocean or lake by continental shifts, volcanic pressure, and seismic activity which caused oceans that once covered land to recede, and lakes that once existed to vanish leaving vast resources of soft rich diatomaceous sediment. Hence, the name Diatomaceous Earth is derived. Other names that have historically been applied to Diatomaceous Earth include diatomite, tripolite, infusorial earth, and kieselghur. Diatomite appears on the ground as a bright white to off-white soft rock that resembles an undulating landscape of snow that can expand across hundreds of acres in area. If you kicked at a mound of the soft rock, dust would fly up. Or, if you wiped your hands over the surface they would be covered with a fine layer of whitish powder.

Over the last 75 years, modern man has commercially mined deposits in the western states of USA (California, Nevada, Oregon, and Washington) which supply over 50 percent of the world's production of Diatomite. DE is produced in about 29 countries including: Canada, France, Denmark, Iceland, Soviet and Czech Republics, Turkey, Iran, Algeria, Kenya, Morocco, Japan, South Korea, China, Mexico, Peru, Argentina, Costa Rica, Chile, Brazil, Columbia, New Zealand, and Australia.

Different mining deposits can reveal varying qualities of DE, some of which occurred during the evolutionary process of becoming diatomite ore, such as with geological pressure, etc. Further, selective mining processes ensure DE is uncontaminated with ash, clay, limestone, salt, microbial spores or other organic debris. Once fine-screened into the powder form, DE has become one of the Earth's greatest natural resources, although it is still not widely known for its precious value in replacing the use of hundreds of chemical pesticides on the market today. DE can also be used as an *anti-caking agent* and nutritional supplement in animal feed, and as a natural soil amender, to name just a couple of the uses found in the following chapters.

The ONLY grade of DE which is safe to use for these specified purposes in the home, garden, orchard, or around farm animals and birds, etc., is from natural-milled, primarily fresh water, unheated amorphous (non crystalline) sources. It is commonly referred to as *food grade,* but unfortunately, this description is not allowed by law to be placed on labels of appropriate food grade quality DE products.

The grade which is NOT SAFE for uses described herein, is from high crystalline and high heated sources (also known as *straight* or *flux calcined*) silicon dioxide, regardless of whether from marine or freshwater. This latter source of DE is commonly used for industrial purposes, such as in paint fillers and filtering aids for pools and aquariums. Note: Chapter Eight is very important to read regarding high crystalline cautions, and choosing the right kind of DE to use.

Will we ever run out of Diatomaceous Earth? Some researchers have said there is enough in USA for about 150 years. However, millions of years into the future, man will still find a treasure of uses for the diatoms that live today and drop to the lake or ocean floor.

Now, if you simply want to get on with learning how to use DE, please move on to Chapter Two. But, for those who are captured and fascinated with this ancient marvel of a modern day insecticide, (which has mostly escaped notice by the majority of society), or if you are joining the growing numbers of those who prefer to *go green* and help save our planet, health, animals and children from disease by toxic peril, you may be interested to learn more about the background of this safer alternative.

Rediscovery Of The Diatom & The Classification Chaos: *Is Diatomaceous Earth (DE) Animal Or Vegetable?*

Diatom collecting became a serious pursuit in the early 1800's. After various ocean vessels dragged in plankton nets, each of their findings resulted in many different names being given to the same species. Reclassification started in the early 19th century when a German microscopist, J. D. Moller, spent 15 years mounting 4,026 different species of diatoms onto a single slide in a space the size of a postage stamp.

An article written by Richard Hoover, a diatom explorer and microscopist, stated in the June 1979 issue of National Geographic, that he became transfixed when he saw a rare slide at the Henri Von Heurck Museum, in Antwerp, Belgium. When adding water to diatoms that had been dried on paper in 1834, he said, "I was astonished to see them revive and swim after nearly 150 years in slumber." Since then, he patiently mounted his own collection of individual diatoms onto slides, using a hog's eyelash mounted onto a toothpick.

The humble diatom does indeed have some amazing and unusual features. When an early pioneer of microscopy, Anton Von Leeuwenhoek discovered the diatom in 1702, he thought they were tiny animals. Indeed, from the studies of the German diatomist, Gerhard Drebes, diatoms are capable of asexual reproduction, where the nucleus splits and divides into two, and sexual reproduction when two diatoms come together, enveloping themselves in a gel and fertilizing one of three eggs that share chromosomes.

Diatoms also exhibit other animal-like behavior, unlike other types of algae. By extracting and ingesting the silica from the water then skillfully weaving a beautiful glassy structure around themselves, they create microscopic architectural type masterpieces for support, locomotion and protection. These tiny opalescent diatoms often resemble minute porous honeycomb-like filter canisters, cylindrical in shape and similar in composition to the opal gemstone.

There are more than 25,000 different species of diatoms, each with a dazzling variety of shapes: pinwheels, stars, spirals, barrels, cylinders, circles, pill boxes, sand dollars and sunbursts. Like fingerprints, no two diatoms are the same. Diatoms vary widely in size, but the largest measure only a millimeter across. To the naked eye their appearance is usually unimpressive, but under the microscope they provide a kaleidoscope of fascination.

In their multitudes, just one pint of water may contain ten million of these microscopic chlorophyll-contained specks of protoplasm, which both give off oxygen to the atmosphere and provide food in the ocean or lake. Together in their teeming trillions, diatoms produce about 80 percent of the world's oxygen to support life—an enormous contribution to our atmosphere. Hence, scientists have classified the tiny diatom as a plant.

Accidental Discovery Of Diatomaceous Earth's Insecticidal Properties

Long before man was first chased by a flea, birds and animals were strutting in Diatomaceous Earth (DE), flapping their wings and fluffing themselves in dust baths to get rid of lice. For millions of years, animals have rolled in dust, habitually ridding themselves of the nit picking, pesky problems caused by fleas, ticks, lice and other similarly irritating annoyances. Since the Chinese and Egyptians use of DE some 4,000 years ago to preserve grain, nuts, legumes and seeds from disintegration by moisture, mold and pests, over time, especially since the advent of chemicals, people lost touch with its benefits until recent scientists resurfaced the potentials, some quite by accident.

A small-time inventor of synthetic turquoise and terrazzo gemstones, Louis de Lisle made jewelry using DE in a primitive Phoenix, Arizona, workshop in 1958. Neil Clark, a dairyman who frequently watched the chemist at work in his laboratory made a surprising observation which brought about a resurgence of interest in DE. To their amazement, on the days when white diatomite was hammer-milled to a powder, the dust rose and either repelled or killed the hoards of flies that plagued them. So, together, these men started investigational tests and studies. The course of events was so overwhelmingly positive, that Clark ended his 30-year career as a dairyman, becoming president of Phoenix Gems. Since then, DE has resulted in a million-dollar industry.

Many hundreds of tests later and armed with data on the deadly effect of diatomaceous dust on insects, it was deemed important to ascertain whether there were any detrimental effects on warm-blooded animals. With a Food and Drug Administration (FDA) approval, Dr. E. Bertke, a zoologist at Arizona State University, was commissioned to do further testing. Results confirmed by the Bureau of Biological and Physical Sciences of the US Department of Health, Education and Welfare concluded that Diatomaceous Earth was harmless to warm-blooded animals. In fact, the test animals even gained weight. Scientists suggested, "Diatomaceous Earth may have some stimulating effect which could be due to trace elements necessary for cell growth and metabolism."

This was great news to Clark, who had always been concerned about chemical insecticide poison residues in milk. He said, "If this diatomaceous dust is not a poison, it represents the most important breakthrough in centuries." Clark discovered Diatomaceous Earth worked with maximum effectiveness as an insecticide only when milled and screened in a particular manner. Soon, the FDA verified that, while Diatomaceous Earth was entirely harmless to humans and other warm-blooded life, it was lethal to insects, having a 98 percent repellency factor—remarkable when compared to 60 percent, which is the normal amount considered acceptable for a chemical insecticide.

Bugs Overpowered By A Simple Algae

A simple living diatom, minding its own business of photosynthesis in the vast prehistoric aquatics of the earth, never hurt anyone. Wouldn't even hurt a flea—that is, not until long after the diatom is dead. Have you ever heard of any plant laying dead and dormant for 25 million years, then resurfacing, and while still dead, protecting us against most of man's dreaded insects? Creepy crawlies such as cockroaches, scorpions, fire ants and termites among dozens of other bugs, won't daunt the diatom—they will eventually succumb.

Upon physical contact, bugs are helplessly put out of action for good. That's good news for the gardener who struggles against these pesky nuisances to grow food for survival; the housekeeper who doesn't like to serve insect larvae with her rice; the little boy who hates to be bitten by bed bugs; the farmer whose beasts won't fatten because they're full of parasites inside and out, and more.

Springing from such needs of man with his technological interventions, the simple diatom, even after being dead since the dinosaur ages, poses the most lethal threat to bugs while simultaneously bringing the kindest benefits to the earth. Nothing can compare to the humble diatom on its journey once it is eaten by a cat, dog, hog, cow, horse, or ostrich. As it travels through miles of putrid bowels, it tames the stench of stool as a natural deodorizer, and also kills a string of parasites and larvae in its wake. Only then to be rewarded by being unceremoniously dumped out in the host's manure, where it goes on to kill fly larvae. Eventually the diatom is trampled down into the mulch, where it continues to nourish the earth with one of the world's most natural and potent forms of trace minerals. As a natural fertilizer, DE stimulates growth and metabolism in beasts as well as plants! This dead diatom is quite a phenomenal piece of work, having the added potential of making our environment a more hospitable and healthier place to live.

Insects Die By Dehydration & No Harmful Chemicals

The method of how DE kills bugs is by mechanical action—not by chemical poisoning. Amorphous Diatomaceous Earth is a natural desiccant, (dries out or dehydrates). In short, DE works by drying bugs up. The diatom's lattice-like architecture creates pores. These pores create a large surface area, which gives the dust its absorptive quality, capable of absorbing 1½ times its weight in water. With this special capacity to absorb both oil and water through the vast number of pores, DE soaks up the protective waxy outer covering on the insect, which then allows body fluids to be absorbed or depleted, and organ functions to stop, with possible interference of the breathing mechanism.

Some old schools of thought, not agreed upon by all miners and manufacturers of DE, believe that microscopic razor sharp silica crystals (shards) abrade or scratch the outer layer of the bug causing the loss of body fluids. This old notion still finds its way into the literature and onto websites.

The current authoritative texts confirm that the "mode of action" of DE, causes the insects to die by dehydration. Serious investigators have long understood DE's mechanical action on insects as follows: "All fossil diatoms are porous, and it is this porosity or specific surface (square meters per gram) that confers them their insecticidal value," (Ebeling 1971). Some brands of DE have a higher number of pores per diatom, which they say is the key to its higher efficiency as an insecticide without the need to add any other ingredients to improve its performance.

Death comes in an average of 12 hours. Some insects such as

carpenter ants have been seen by the author to die within seconds and other types of ants within an hour or two after venturing into Diatomaceous Earth. The exception is for those bugs that have a constant source of food and water to replenish their fluid loss. These wounded bugs will be distracted by spending much of their time replacing fluids, however, as long as they remain in contact with the dust, they will soon succumb.

DE Is 98 Percent Naturally Bug Repellent

In addition to being an effective non-polluting bug killer, DE is a powerful repellant, acting as a *natural barrier* to fence off unwanted bugs for as long as it remains on the treated surface. Bugs tend to stay away longer from a treated area. As long as DE is present, and the more it is used, an environment is being created which makes insects feel unwelcome. Even bugs that don't make physical contact with the dust seem to sense DE when diffused in the vicinity. Possibly it interferes with their breathing mechanics, causing enough dis-comfort to send them scurrying in the opposite direction. Flies seem to disappear where dust rises into the air, while bees tend to avoid blossoms treated with Diatomaceous Earth.

While there is at least a 90-day beneficial residual effect with the use of DE (in areas where it is not washed away), reapplications are suggest-ed at least four or more times a year for complete year-round control. The thousands of farmers and gardeners who pride themselves on their prize organic crops will probably make weekly DE dustings.

Properly prepared and applied, Diatomaceous Earth is capable of killing almost every kind of insect with which it comes in contact. Being significantly less expensive to produce than many chemical insecticides, DE is rapidly becoming a safe and economical choice with a built-in bonus of providing many other benefits to the earth, man, birds and animals.

Where Is Diatomaceous Earth (DE) Available?

DE is usually sold as a "horticultural helper" in some garden supply stores, hardware stores, nurseries, health food stores, pet supply stores, veterinary clinics, franchise distributorships, online and mail order.

If you don't want to apply Diatomaceous Earth yourself and prefer a professional exterminator to use it where you live, play, work, or go to school, you can search online or in the newspapers, or yellow pages for a chemical-free Pest Control Operator (PCO) in your area. Due to their own concern of environmental pollution and increasing public demand from health-minded customers, many PCO's have added an alternative "chem-free" or "green" division using Diatomaceous Earth. In USA the best of these PCO's offer a 100 percent Diatomaceous Earth product as their insecticide of choice known by the label as a "crawling insect killer." PCO's have all the right apparatus to treat wall voids, attics, basements and other inaccessible regions of homes and other buildings with Diatomaceous Earth in order to eliminate insects. In these areas Diatomaceous Earth's effectiveness is indefinite.

The author used a local chem-free PCO in Austin, Texas, to spray DE all over the attic of their home which was haunted by scorpions. The baby scorpions died within a few days. Although it took a few weeks for a few scorpions to eventually come into contact with the DE dust as some of them hid under the insulation, they eventually all died and stopped coming down through the fan fixture openings in the ceiling. A neighbor who also had scorpions in their attic heard of the author's success and got some DE. They applied it around the attic and under the house by blowing it with a fan through a cardboard funnel. Of course the best time to apply DE to an attic and under the house is while it is being built.

2

Diatomaceous Earth (DE) Uses As A Safer Home & Garden Insecticide

Important Caution:

In accordance with the officially recommended 1997 OSHA safety standard, all tips in this chapter suggest using only *food grade* Diatomaceous Earth, which is pure amorphous "non-crystalline" silicon dioxide, with 0.1 percent ($^1/_{10th}$ of 1 percent) or less "crystal-line" silica and no additives.

Food Grade

Diatomaceous Earth is Also Known As:

* *Grain Storage Protectant*

* *Animal Feed Additive*

* *Anti-Caking Agent*

* *Inert Carrier*

20 NOVELTY HOME USES FOR DE

How To Use DE As A Natural Deodorizer

To deodorize a drawer, cupboard or closet with DE: Recycle an empty box that is suitable for the size and type of space. Put some DE into it, (doesn't have to be full, but enough to be effective). Tape on the lid, then punch several ¼ to ½ inch holes in the top. For a drawer, try using a 2 to 3 inch match stick box or chocolate box. For a closet, try 2 to 3 cupfuls of DE in a shoe box, or any other kind of sturdy container which can handle holes in the lid.

To deodorize a garbage can with DE: Sprinkle Diatomaceous Earth in the bottom of the garbage can. Helps to deodorize and kills bugs and larvae on contact when added to a dry can.

To deodorize the kitty litter box, keep it dry and help prevent flies with DE: Diatomaceous Earth is odorless, so it should not deter cats from using the litter box. Since the litterbox will smell fresher with the use of DE, cats are more likely to use it for a bit longer before a change is needed. Use an old spatula to mix a handful of DE with the kitty litter. DE not only deodorizes but also absorbs moisture twice its own weight. Be careful to use only pure food grade DE (Anti-Caking Agent) or Grain Storage Protectant (with no other chemical or natural additives).

To prevent odors when vacuuming and to kill bugs in the bag: Place 2 tablespoons of Diatomaceous Earth in the vacuum bag with each new change and again when half full. The DE will not only deodorize, but also kill any bugs and larvae picked up.

To deodorize a bread bin with DE: To keep bread fresh and prevent mold avoid placing hot steamy bread in the bin. Thoroughly wash the entire inside of the bread bin in hot soapy water. Dry, then spray or wipe with straight vinegar and leave until dry if there was mold. Place a low wire mesh cake stand in the bottom of the bin to raise the bread up and allow the air to circulate underneath. Make a small breathable pouch of DE out of a clean cotton handkerchief or a couple layers of dry cheesecloth, or muslin potpourri bag. Place 3 to 4-tablespoons of DE in the center then tie all four corners closed with a bread twist wire. Place the bag under the mesh stand of bread to absorb moisture and odors. The DE can be re-used by drying out from time-to-time in a flat pan in the oven (without a fan or the muslin cloth) on low heat for about 20 minutes.

To deodorize the refrigerator using DE: DE can be used in much the same way as baking soda to banish odors. Leave an open box or jar of DE in the refrigerator and freezer. Change the contents as often as you need to change baking soda.

To deodorize footwear using DE: Place some DE into the ends of two knee-high nylon stockings, or cut a pair off panty hose at knee level. Fill part of the stocking feet with DE, then tie a knot in the top, and also wherever there are any holes. Place the stockings inside the shoes or boots. Leave 8 to 48 hours or until used again. Alternatively, in the absence of stockings, lightly sprinkle food grade DE into the bottom of footwear and leave 1 to 2 hours or overnight. Turn upside down. Vigorously tap on the sole to remove all DE before wearing. Wipe the remainder of the powder out with a cloth or towel. DE dries the skin so it may be necessary to wear socks after this treatment. DE also helps retard fungal growth.

How To Use Diatomaceous Earth (DE) As A Natural Cleaner & Absorbent

To make DE soft scrub cleaner: Mix *food grade* Diatomaceous Earth (DE) with a few drops of vinegar or lemon juice and vegetable oil to make a paste. Add a small squirt of liquid vegetable oil soap. Stir with a fork until creamy.

To remove motor oil from garage floor, driveway or parking space using DE: To start, make sure the area is free of water. Pick a fine day for this chore. Turn garden sprinklers off. Using a flour sieve, food colander, jar, or coffee can with holes punched in the lid, pour DE into the container and sprinkle enough to liberally and completely cover the stain. Leave the DE powder to soak up the oil for 4 to 24 hours, then remove the excess with an old metal spatula, paint scraper or dustpan, then carefully dispose.

Repeat if necessary. Wash any further stain color with a bucket of hot water and a squirt of biodegradable dish washing liquid. Scrubbing to a good lather with a hard bristle brush or long handled broom will help to remove the rest of the dark greasy stain. Just as a note of interest, DE is used to contain large industrial oil spills. DE can absorb moisture twice its weight.

To remove grease or oil from a carpet with DE: Keep the area dry. Sprinkle food grade DE onto the stain, allow the powder to absorb overnight, and then vacuum clean.

To remove grease and dirt from non-washable wall-paper using DE: Rub Diatomaceous Earth on the spot, wait to absorb the grease then brush off.

To remove muddy footprints from carpet with DE: Sprinkle DE powder on wet or dry mud spots. Gently brush with a stiff broom into the carpet without rubbing, then vacuum after 1 to 2 hours or whenever the powder and mud appears dry.

To polish copper bottom pots with DE: Dip a cloth into vinegar, wring out very tightly, then dip into the DE powder and rub it on the pot dry, or use as a paste mixed with just 2 or 3 drops of vinegar or lemon juice.

To polish silver with DE: Mix some DE powder with 2 to 3 drops of water or milk to make a thick, creamy consistency. Apply it like any silver cleaner, rubbing with a cloth and wash well. DE is a natural abrasive. Try rubbing on dry DE powder to shine silver.

To make a gentle silver cleaning paste: DE has a natural and gentle abrasive quality. The trick is to not make it too wet. Mix DE with either a few drops of vinegar, lemon, milk or salad oil, just enough to make a thick creamy consistency. Or, mix all these ingredients together with the DE to form a thick paste. Dip a part of a moistened clean cloth into the paste and rub on the item. Rinse well. Silver tarnish can also be removed simply by rubbing on dry DE powder with the fingers or a cloth.

To retard silver flatware from tarnishing while not in use:
When there is no time to polish regularly, try wrapping silver in plastic, cellophane wrap or aluminum foil with a very light sprinkling of DE to absorb any moisture. Wash well before using. Save the DE to reuse. Or, fold a few spoonfuls of DE into the center of either a 12-inch square piece of muslin or thin cotton fabric or handkerchief. Tie the corners. Or recycle the foot end of a clean nylon stocking. Place a few spoonfuls of DE powder inside, tie a knot in the top, and place the pouch inside the silverware box.

How To Use Diatomaceous Earth (DE) As
A Natural Preservative

How to preserve paper products from mold, mildew and destruction by silverfish and book lice: Food grade DE absorbs moisture and acts as a mold and mildew inhibitor. Use a fine sprinkling of DE to preserve paper products, especially precious collections and documents. DE helps prevent moisture and stickiness between layers or folds of paper such as old printed articles, patterns, books, antique or collector items like comics, cards, maps, journals, and newspapers, etc. Use DE in the basement, attic, cellar, storage shed, storage bin, warehouse, workshop, containers, or any dark and damp place wherever there are stacks or folded layers.

Apply DE to preserve paper products as follows: Use a dust mask and eye goggles while using DE. Pour DE into a spice jar, pepper shaker, jar or can with holes punched in the lid, sieve or colander. Then very lightly sprinkle the powder onto both sides of the pages, and between folds and layers. Leave DE in place if the items are to be kept in long-term storage, or leave a day or two to absorb moisture then remove. DE can be placed just in the bottom of a storage container to absorb moisture and prevent old mildew smells. Since DE can be drying to skin, be careful to wash powder from hands. Apply hand cream if needed.

How to keep playing cards from sticking: Sprinkle DE onto a soft cloth and wipe over both sides of the playing cards removing all excess.

How to prevent stored and folded plastic tablecloths from sticking and molding: Picnic and plastic tablecloths can be treated in the same way as paper products as mentioned above.

How to preserve roses and leaves: Preserve those precious memories and make a dried arrangement—perhaps a gift from your own garden. Using an airtight plastic container, cover the bottom with Diatomaceous Earth. This will act as a natural drying agent (desiccant). Then gently place dry flowers or leaves on top of the DE in a single layer. Take care to not allow the edges to touch each other. Carefully place a light layering of DE on top. Place the lid on and seal with tape if the container is not airtight. Leave undisturbed for 3 days. Keeping the container upright, open the cover and turn the flowers or leaves over if not thoroughly dried out. Handle carefully as petals and leaves will be brittle. Seal the lid tight again and leave for another 3 days. Dried leaves and flowers when covered in the DE may become too brittle to remove the dust completely. To avoid leaving a milky appearance, separate the layers of DE from the item to be dried with cotton handkerchiefs.

How to preserve stored onions and flower bulbs from mold: Store in a mesh onion bag, nylon stocking, cotton sock, pillowcase or muslin. Lightly sprinkle with Diatomaceous Earth to keep dry and mold-free until planting time. Hang the bag in a dry place in order for air to flow around the items.

Insecticidal Uses For Diatomaceous Earth (DE) In The Home And Garden

Careful housekeeping helps keep bugs away: The battle of the bug is constantly on the mind of the average homemaker. Not only do insects find their way in from the outdoors, but every time someone goes to the grocery store and brings back a box or sack, they may be carrying a live weevil, roach or larvae (eggs). Even the most fastidious housekeeper will occasionally find a roach, and where there is one, there are likely to be more. Don't invite bugs in the first place. (See *Cockroaches, fleas* and *weevils* etc., below for more in-depth and specific preventative housekeeping details).

Application methods: how and where to apply DE: Be sure to buy only pure 100 percent food grade DE without additives and which has less than 0.1 percent ($^1/_{10th}$ of 1 percent) crystalline silica as per the 1997 OSHA recommendations.

Although food grade DE is not poisonous, wear gloves if handling directly, as DE can dry out the skin. As with any dust, wear a mask to avoid breathing airborne particles and goggles to protect the eyes from dust irritation during the application of DE. Repeat after rain if DE washes away. Asthmatics and those with other chronic respiratory ailments can apply DE outdoors as a liquid spray to reduce the dust nuisance.

Any dusting equipment on the market (often available from hardware or garden supply stores) such as small hand dusters, pumps or back packs units may be used to apply DE uniformly and liberally on any area. Some DE comes in a squeezable can with a handy tip, which can be used as a crack and crevice nozzle for use in tight spaces. DE can be placed in a squeeze-type mustard or ketchup bottle that has a handy crack and crevice nozzle. A colander, flour sieve or coffee can with holes punched in the lid is useful for easy sprinkling of DE over a wide area such as a carpet, floor, patio, lawn, attic, basement, pet run, yard or vehicle. Use a firm broom to spread the DE. *(See Chapter Five on Tools and Methods of Application, which includes how to make a liquid solution).*

DE acts as a barrier or repellant to "fence out" bugs from where they like to hide, making it uninhabitable as long as the dust remains dry and in place. Treat open spaces with a strip of DE or a light sprinkling on, around, or beneath stoves, refrigerators, dishwashers, sinks, cabinets, counters, garbage cans, furniture, sewer pipes, drains, attics, basements, porches, patios, doorsteps, floors stairs, utility closets, rooms, suspended ceilings, storage rooms, crawl spaces, moldings, window and door frames, electrical boxes, corners in closets, cabinets, shelves, windowsills and ledges under drawers. Work DE into carpets with a stiff brush or broom, taking care to apply a fine layer beneath loose rugs and doormats, etc. Apply DE to mattresses and bed frames—very effective against mites and bed-bugs. After 12 to

48 hours brush off well outdoors before using.

For baseboard treatment, backs of cabinets and in cracks and crevices, lightly coat the area at the rate of 4-oz. per 1,000 sq. feet. Remember that DE is a *contact* natural insecticide, so direct application on the insect, or application where the insect will physically come in contact with the product will give the best results.

Outside the home, apply DE to the foundation where dust will remain dry. Dust layers in wood piles, around pools, concrete cracks, eave vents, under rocks and brick piles, or anywhere else there may be an insect problem.

Out of sight—out of mind. DE does not necessarily need to be cleaned up. It will continue working to either repel or kill bugs after just a one-time application when a fine layer of 100 percent or food grade DE remains unobtrusive and out of reach. Apply DE behind appliances or cabinets, in cracks, crevices and corners, drawers, garbage cans, attics, basements, beneath the house, under door and windowsills, in mesh screen door and window tracks, and on pantry and food cellar shelves, etc. Amazingly, as long as sufficient DE stays dry and in place, it will continue to be effective regardless of how many years the powder remains there.

When spraying plants, be sure to apply DE to both upper and lower leaf surfaces to obtain the best results. An electrostatic ionizer will ensure liquid or powder DE polarizes and clings to the underside of leaves. *(See Chapter Six, Tools and Methods for how to use DE as a liquid spray or "slurry").*

A-Z Plants To Treat With Natural Diatomaceous Earth (DE) Insecticide

Asparagus: asparagus beetle.

Beans: aphids, leafhoppers, whitefly, Mexican bean beetle, 12-spotted cucumber beetle.

Broccoli, Cabbage, Brussels Sprouts, Cauliflower: aphids, cabbage looper, cross-striped cabbageworm, diamond back moth larvae, flea beetle, harlequin bug, imported cabbageworm, stink bug.

Celery: green peach aphid, cabbage looper, leaf tier.

Corn: ear worm, budworm.

Cotton: armyworm, bollworm.

Cranberries: fireworms, leafhopper.

Eggplants: blister beetle, Colorado potato beetle, flea beetle, green peach aphids.

Grains (wheat, barley, oats, sorghum): armyworms, range caterpillar, midges.

Lettuce: cabbage looper, green peach aphid, diamond back moth larvae, imported cabbageworm.

Mustard Greens, Kale, Collards, Turnips: imported cabbageworm, diamondback caterpillar, aphids, cabbage looper.

Pasture Grass: armyworm, cutworms, range caterpillar, other caterpillars.

Peanuts: armyworms, cutworms, cabbage looper, stink bug.

Pecan: pecan weevil.

Peas (field): armyworms, caterpillars, pea curculio.

Peppers: green peach aphid.

Potatoes: aphids, Colorado potato beetle, flea beetle, leafhopper.

Peaches: peach borer.

Radishes: aphid, flea beetle.

Soy Bean: armyworm, cabbage looper, Mexican bean beetle.

Spinach: aphids, cabbage looper, webworm.

Tobacco: hornworm, fleas.

Tomatoes: green peach aphids, Colorado potato beetle, stink bug, flea beetle.

Ornamentals: (ie., African violets, asters, azaleas, begonias, camellias, carnations, chrysanthemums, dahlias, dogwood, geraniums, gladioli): flea beetle and leafhopper.

A-Z Bugs To Treat With Diatomaceous Earth (DE)

DE is especially effective against bugs that live in close association with humans, such as cockroaches, lice, silverfish, mites, ants, flies, earwigs, slugs, termites, houseflies, spiders, bedbugs, fleas, beetles, moths and other crawling insects. The list of bugs below is not all-inclusive. Diatomaceous Earth will work to eliminate almost any bug when any of these methods are used below.

To minimize killing beneficial insects during application such as lady bugs and pollinating bees, treat outdoor plants in the early morning or late evening when the count is low. Spray plants first with a fine mist including under the leaves to encourage the DE to stick better, and then use a puffer applicator to apply dry DE powder on the leaves including the undersides. Or, make a liquid solution and use a spray applicator. Although DE can still impede and even kill bugs while wet, this natural substance works more efficiently once it dries. (*See Chapter Five for tools and methods for many ways to apply DE, electrostatic ionizers for making DE cling to surfaces, and how to make a liquid solution*).

ANTS

To keep ants from trashcans sprinkle or spray DE around the outside and bottom of the can to act as a barrier to fence them out. Sprinkle or spray DE around the house foundation to keep bugs from crawling inside.

To treat small lawn and carpet areas for ants: Pour DE powder from the original container into a flour sifter or large colander, or any other mesh-type applicator. Walk around the area to be treated while tapping the side of the applicator to sprinkle a fine layer of DE through the mesh. DE may be applied to ant mounds, paths and lawns as a liquid solution (slurry) with a hand held sprayer, backpack spray pump or hose-end sprayer. The solution becomes more effective once dry, however, many users have success with DE while still wet. Harder and thicker bodied bugs such as fireants, cockroaches and scorpions will succumb quicker in dry DE as it is more absorptive, and the bug is not able to rehydrate itself in the absence of water.

Large lawn ant treatment: Mix 6-pounds of DE with water to fill a 50-gallon agitator tank. This concentrated mix is best applied with a hose-end sprayer, or high pressure, agriculture-type boom sprayer. Application should be set to deliver at the amount of 3-pounds per acre.

To treat ant mounds: Mix 4-tablespoons of DE to 1-gallon of water. For larger areas and multiple mounds, mix 1-pound of DE to 25-gallons of water. As an option, add 1-teaspoon of liquid dish soap to each gallon of this DE "slurry" solution. Using a cone shaped ream tool, funnel out the center of the ant mound, or poke a hole in the center with a stick. Mix the DE solution well by agitating the container again, allowing no residue to settle on the bottom. Trickle the DE solution into the hole until full. For small ant mounds, or smaller numbers of mounds, 1 to 2 pints of this mixture may suffice. While covering ant mounds, include a 6-inch surrounding area. Small ants will burrow deep and build satellite mounds, so they may require a few applications to be completely eliminated. Be persistent until they disappear. It may take a couple of good applications to a mound to get rid of bigger ants.

Treating satellite ant mounds: If the queen ant is not killed, a satellite mound will pop up. During the cooler temperatures of morning and evening, the queen is closer to the top of the mound which makes this the best time to treat. As the temperature warms, the queen moves down deeper into the mound and can escape via new deeper tunnels to form a new satellite mound. Several weeks may be required to eliminate the colony completely. New satellite mounds can appear as survivors migrate away from the originally-treated areas. Therefore, it is a good idea to make a DE dust barrier strip around your entire property to help stop further migration between adjoining neighbors.

To keep ants off fruit trees and buildings: Using the liquid solution (slurry) as above, paint on exterior surfaces of walls and tree trunks with a brush or any spray applicator. Or, use a puffer applicator and apply a thin veil of dry DE. To keep ants from entering buildings, apply a thin line of DE as a barrier around buildings, entry points and at the threshold of entrances. DE will need replacing if washed away by watering, rain or wind.

Fire Ant Control

Drench individual mounds using a solution of 4-tablespoons of DE to 1-gallon of water, or 1-pound of DE to 25-gallons of water.

Method #1

For ant mounds larger than 13-inches in diameter triple the recommended dosage above. Mix the DE solution well until no residue is seen in the bottom to attain even and adequate distribution. Apply with a spray can, hose-end sprayer, or backpack spray pump as follows: For best results apply the DE solution (or powder) in cool weather, or in early morning or late evening hours when the temperature is generally between 65 and 80 degrees F. Saturate a 6-inch perimeter of the mound, working toward the center in a circular motion. After the mound is saturated, inject the mixture into the mound cavity in several different places until the DE solution puddles on the surface. Reapply as necessary to maintain contact until all fire ants are eliminated. Fire ants are hardier than most other types of ants. As with many chemical treatments, it may take a few hours, or even days to be successful, and may even take repeated treatments. It is important to treat satellite mounds—(see below).

Method #2

Stir ant mound with a rake, hoe or broom handle, or level it to expose and agitate ants. Apply a layer of either dry DE powder or pour the solution liberally on immediate area, contacting as many ants as possible. This is not a poison, so ants must come into physical contact with DE to die. Repeat as necessary after rain, or when new mounds or ants reappear, especially before they begin to rebuild strength in their colony.

To treat ant trails: First clean up and remove any food source that may be attracting ants. A squeeze type accordion puffer bottle with a crack and crevice applicator is useful for applying DE especially under heavy appliances without having to move them, and to cover narrow, deep or hard to reach places. Improvising with a mustard bottle or flour sieve can be practical for using DE powder. Outside the home remove debris or sprinkle a thin layer of DE beneath. Treat entry points (including windowsills, doorways, cupboards and wall cracks).

To treat ants underneath the house or in the attic: If it is impossible to get under the house into the crawl space, wearing a dust mask and goggles, blow DE under the house through the ventilation openings. Put some DE powder on a shovel and use a leaf blower to direct it through the vent. If the dust scatters before reaching the vent, make a cardboard funnel as a shield, big enough to insert the shovel into, then blow the DE through. As long as the powder remains there and stays dry, it will be effective for years.

To stop ants bugging pets: Diatomaceous Earth works well as a non-toxic insecticide in dog runs. According to Howard Garrett, a radio gardening host, Dallas landscape architect and author of ***Plants of the Metroplex III*** and ***The Organic Landscape Manual,*** individual mounds can be knocked out with vinegar and DE (a ¼ -cup of DE in 1-gallon of vinegar) poured into the center of the mound. Ant trails may be treated with dry food grade DE powder that can be left in place.

BEDBUGS

Increasing world travel has brought these pests back. Take the bed frame apart then apply Diatomaceous Earth to the joints, cracks and crevices. Some puffer or squeeze type applicator bottles come with a crack and crevice nozzle. If the frame is hollow, dust the interior of the framework. Be sure to dust folds, bindings, joints, edges, as well as under the bed. Dust the mattress (using only pure food grade DE without additives and with less than 0.1 percent crystalline silica). Leave DE on the mattress a couple of days, vacuum off well and make the bed as usual. Thoroughly wash all used linens. There is no need to wash DE off the bed frame wherever it remains out of sight. Treat all cracks and crevices in the room. Although safe for this use, food grade DE can dry the skin. Caution: Do not use swimming pool or industrial grade DE.

CARPET BEETLES

Thoroughly dust with DE along baseboards, under furniture, on carpet and rug edges and underneath, in closets, on shelving, or wherever carpet beetles are seen or suspected to inhabit. Use a colander, sieve, or a coffee can or jar with holes in the lid to lightly dispense DE over a wide area.

COCKROACHES

Rule number one—avoid inviting roaches to dine: Always maintain good clean housekeeping habits. Cover or put food put away as soon as the meal is over. Regularly and carefully clean up all food spills, crumbs, scraps and garbage.

Curb the cockroaches attraction to pet food: Pet food left lying around will attract cockroaches so clean the surrounding area and bowl each time the pet eats. Always keep dried pet food stored in an airtight container. Also mix DE *(without additives such as pyrethrum as per the Grains formula)* into bags of stored dried pet food. DE is odorless and as a natural deodorizer, it should not turn pets off their food. By protecting the pet's food, the animal may in time begin to show better health and a shinier coat due to absorption of the added trace mineral nutrients and the ability of DE to help eliminate worms and parasites from the gut. Keep plenty of water available for the pet.

How and where to apply DE to eliminate cockroaches:
DE powder can be sprinkled over any surface where cockroaches hide with a flour sieve, saltshaker, colander or a jar with holes poked in the lid. Alternatively, use a crack and crevice nozzle such as an accordion type puffer bottle, pest pistol, or a mustard bottle to squeeze a line of dust into hard-to-reach places. Puff or sprinkle a thin layer of DE around and under appliances such as the refrigerator, stove and dishwasher, beneath and behind cabinets, in the pantry, on shelves around food storage bags and containers, around pipes, and also in and around the garbage can. Don't expect cockroaches to drop dead at your feet, but DE does have a high success rate with eradicating them, even after a couple of days. There is no need to clean up DE wherever it remains out of sight. Leave DE in place and it will do its job for years as long as there is a fine layer for adequate coverage, and as long as it stays dry.

Fix all water leaks: After a cockroach comes into contact with DE it will sooner or later become dehydrated. However, cockroaches will attempt to rehydrate at any possible water source. Fix leaks and mop up spilled or stagnant water. If this is not entirely or immediately possible and water remains, it helps to apply a thicker layer of DE over the area and to repeat the process more often. As long as there has been enough physical contact with the DE, eventually the substance will destroy the bug's organs and interfere with the ability to feed, digest, reproduce and move.

Cockroaches do not develop resistance to DE: Cockroaches treated with synthetic toxic chemicals will become increasingly difficult to eradicate due to development of resistance and mutation of genes. However, cockroaches cannot develop immunity to DE as it is not a chemical. DE eradicates by mechanical means with the dehydrating action of the natural opalescent silicon dioxide. For this reason DE has been used in a Nevada city sewer to successfully eradicate cockroaches. DE was blown into open manholes. Soon dead roaches floating on sewer water flooded into the disposal plant by the thousands. Just one treatment can last up to 6 months, even in places with a lot of moisture that could slow down the dehydration and dying process.

FLEAS

The life cycle of a flea has four stages of development that spans over 14 to 21 days: egg, larva, pupa and adult. The flea's favorite temperature is 65 to 80 degrees F. with 70 percent humidity. Even if there is a hot summer, (over 95 degrees), fleas may breed prolifically inside the house where the temperature is lower.

Where fleas can be found: Flea eggs far outnumber adult fleas, so the secret of control is to eliminate the eggs. The best way to control flea larvae in carpet is frequent vacuuming, or better still steam cleaning. Once flea eggs hatch, the larvae love to lunch on organic debris. Fleas and larvae will survive in decaying plant matter, dead animal matter, dog runs and beds, in automobiles, soft furnishings, carpets, trash, under scrap boards, concrete cracks and in grass. Wherever fleas land they thrive and hatch eggs.

Starve fleas out with good housekeeping: Cleaning the environment is a preventative measure that interferes with the insect's breeding cycle and abilities. Regular and frequent sweeping, vacuuming, tidying, and dusting with DE curbs fleas from breeding, especially where pets sleep, sit or play. Apply DE underneath and on top of doormats, carpets, in and around kennels, bedding, pet runs, garden sheds, garages, automobiles, bird cages, and on porches and patios. (See *Carpet Treatment* below for further instructions).

DE application methods to beat fleas: Apply DE uniformly with a hand held duster, pest pistol, flour sieve, colander, or jar or can with holes punched in the lid. Pay particular attention to dark damp places where animals frequent and bugs hide. You may want to combine other flea-fighting methods in addition to DE applications including using a flea comb. Regularly bathing pets with a mild soap and water solution is far safer and healthier than poisonous dips. Going organic also helps. If the soil on your property is healthy and alive with microorganisms and beneficial insects, they will consume a major source of food that fleas would normally eat, which helps starve these pests out.

The carpet treatment to control fleas: Apply DE lightly and thoroughly to carpets one or two days before vacuuming. If the DE container doesn't come with sprinkle holes in the lid, create your own sprinkler using a spice shaker, flour sieve, colander or coffee can with fine holes punched in the lid. Dust the carpet thoroughly with DE including around the edges and underneath if possible. Dust cracks, edges and ledges near baseboards.

Use approximately 6-oz (8 tablespoons equals approximately 1-oz) per 500 square feet until a light coating of DE is visible on the carpet. With a stiff broom, work DE into the base of the pile. To kill larvae, DE needs to remain on the carpet for 24 to 72 hours. Then vacuum well until the powder is no longer visible on the surface. Reapply DE and vacuum every three to four days for effective control throughout the season and life cycle of the flea. Once DE gets inside the vacuum cleaner it helps to provide another totally unfavorable breeding ground. However, applying DE too thickly on surfaces may overstrain the vacuum cleaner.

As long as this off-white odorless and non-staining non-toxic powder is not a visual problem, DE does not need to be picked up. Leave DE in place for any amount of time, and it will continue to be an effective natural insecticide as long as it remains.

How to apply DE to get rid of fleas on pets: Pure 100 percent food grade DE without additives will not poison the animal when rubbed into the fur. For easier application use a puffer or squeeze-type container with a pop-up squirt nozzle (a ketchup or mustard container will do) or a shaker jar with several holes punched in the lid.

Pay particular attention to body parts that the animal can't reach, such as the top of the head. Carefully place DE on the ears, around the eyes and lip line. Then make a good application to the rear end and around the genitals. Next begin to dust the whole body. Starting at the tail, brush the hair backwards with one hand along the spine while puffing the dust at the base of the hair with the other hand. Move forward towards the back of the head. Turn the animal over and do the belly. Don't forget their armpits, elbows, paws and between the toes.

As long as DE remains in place and is in contact with the animal, it will continue to kill insects and eggs through the whole cycle. If a bath or rain washes the DE off, then reapply if fleas remain. In sensitive animals, observe for signs of drying skin and remove the DE by bathing and brushing after a day or two.

Keep the animal's immune system strong. Unhealthy animals are more susceptible to both fleas and lice. To be successful in eliminating a flea infestation, it is vital that everything is treated thoroughly but lightly, all at the same time—all pets and their hangout areas, the yard, interior of the home, carpets, automobiles, kennel, doormats, porches, patios, pet bedding, grass and even concrete cracks to avoid picking up new eggs and fleas. It can take 1 to 3 days to dehydrate the fleas and larvae. Repeat twice a week for 2 to 3 weeks or longer during flea season.

On damp lawns and garden areas DE will not work as well—it does work, but it's more effective and quicker when the area is dry as insects can keep rehydrating themselves on the available moisture. Combining the use of DE with beneficial parasitic nematodes will ensure better success. It takes 2 to 4 weeks. Since the nematodes will vanish when their entire insect food source is eliminated, repeated applications may be necessary in the warmer months.

For flea infested litters: Some schools of thought caution using DE on or near kittens less than 6 weeks old—this is especially important if the DE has any added ingredients such as pyrethrum or permethrin as these are toxic nerve agents. However the dust alone may irritate newborn kittens' undeveloped lungs causing an asthma type condition especially if used too heavily. Twice a week place kittens and small puppies in a large enough bucket, bowl or pan of food grade DE, then cover them lightly all over, avoiding the eyes. Apply DE to the mother and other pets that come into contact with the litter. Put a light coating of DE in the bedding and litter box. DE deodorizes and absorbs moisture in kitty litter keeping it drier, and also helps kill parasites, worms and larvae in the litter.

How to make a liquid spray DE to eliminate fleas: Add 4 heaped tablespoons of DE to 1-gallon of water in a wide nozzle spray bottle. Shake well before and during the application to prevent DE from settling to the bottom of the container. Spray the yard and any other infested outside area with the DE solution, then wait for it to dry to become more effective. Concentrate on dark damp spots favored by fleas, including grass. This recipe can also be used for eliminating other bugs.

FLIES

Apply DE where flies land on windowsills and frames, around light fixtures and pet areas, on porches and railings, in garages, garbage cans and anywhere else that flies can reach in the home.

Fly control for ranch homes: Farmers, whose houses are close to their barns, can find life much more tolerable with only a few flies instead of an infestation. Using DE labeled as a *Grain Storage Protectant* or *Anti-Caking Agent* this nutritional trace mineral can be added to animal feed at a rate of 2 percent of the weight of the food ration.

Animals fed DE in their diet have a reduction of scours—their manure is drier with fewer odors. DE eliminated by animals or birds goes on to kill fly larvae in their manure, thereby reducing fly breeding and population. Flies will continue to deposit their eggs in the manure as usual, but fewer larvae will survive to adulthood, as they are dehydrated when moving through the DE substance in order to feed. Farmers have reported a noticeable reduction in stable flies within two or three days of the initial treatment.

Aside from reduced fly hatching, DE also has a deodorizing and drying effect on the manure, making housekeeping much easier. Animals are more content and less bothered by flies. Some dairy and hog farmers are also spreading DE in bedding to keep odors drifting towards their homes, and for moisture control. The air smells cleaner so flies are drastically reduced on the entire farm; hence far fewer flies find their way to ranch houses and other farm buildings. *(See Chapter Four on Agriculture for details, methods, and how to apply DE to farm animals, inside large farm buildings, and to cover large acreage).*

GRAIN WEEVILS

(This is a large section. See entire Chapter Three on DE Benefits and Uses in Grain Storage for Humans and Animals).

LICE

DE as a non-toxic alternative to chemical lice treatments:
Some lice are now becoming immune or resistant to chemical treatments and are developing into "superbugs". Further, harsh and toxic chemical lice treatments (including those often prescribed by doctors, found in pharmacies, or recommended by schools) have reportedly caused nerve damage symptoms including seizures, paralysis and other ailments. *(See Chapter Seven—Toxic Chemical Insecticides Harmful To Health).* DE offers a safer and effective alternative, using 100 percent food grade DE with less than 0.1 percent crystalline silica.

Caution: Swimming pool, aquarium or industrial grade DE is extremely hazardous for lice treatments. DO NOT USE. *(See Chapter Eight—Precautions).*

Application methods for treating lice: While using caution to avoid inhaling DE, and closing or covering the eyes, gently sprinkle food grade DE onto dry hair or fur with a spice or saltshaker. Or, use a jar with holes poked in the lid. Use the applicator gently to avoid creating an airborne dust nuisance. Comb the powder through the hair with a metal nit or flea comb. Wrap the head in clear plastic wrap, or put on a tight shower cap and leave overnight. Shampoo DE out of the hair the next morning using the nit comb to remove all the eggs from individual strands. Rinse with a solution of half vinegar and water, and then apply conditioner or oil as DE can be drying to the hair and scalp.

The oil treatment and leave-in conditioner not only replaces moisture, but it also assists in smothering any remaining lice and larvae and helps them loosen their attachment to the hair. Repeat as often as necessary until all signs of lice and eggs are gone. Treat everything and everyone at the same time to prevent re-infestation. Wash all clothing and bed linen. Toss items that cannot be washed, such as pillows, quilts and plush or cloth toys into a hot drier for 20 to 30 minutes. Wrap mattresses in air-tight plastic and leave for 2 to 3 days in the sunlight if possible. Soak combs and brushes in full strength vinegar, or cover with a sprinkling of DE powder and do not use them for 24 to 48 hours.

DE can also be safely applied to carpets, upholstery, car seats, headrests, and on any item that can't be washed where lice may be suspected to thrive. Leave at least 24 hours, preferably 72 hours and then vacuum off.

For lice on animals, use the same methods as for fleas and also see *Chapter Four* for animal pests.

A DE dust bath for bird and hen lice: To get rid of lice on birds, place a big enough bowl or trough of pure food grade DE (without chemical additives) in a pen or cage with the birds. They will soon be naturally attracted and you can enjoy watching the birds leisurely fluff their feathers in the dust bath to kill their own pests. Many ostrich farmers and veterinarians successfully use DE to treat both internal and external parasites. Pure food grade DE leaves no poisonous chemical residues and is harmless to the soil as well as birds. DE can be safely mixed into any litter box, or spread over the roost, and on the floor of birdhouses on top of the manure. As a result, birds will be a more contented and a cackley bunch.

MEALY BUGS

Mealy bugs look like black mold. Small mealy insects found in cavities on developing fruits will cause them to drop off when only half grown. To avoid fruit damage, spray trees with Diatomaceous Earth (DE) mixed with water at the rate of 4-tablespoons of DE to 1-gallon of water, or 1-pound of DE to 25-gallons of water. To apply, use a hose-end sprayer, back pack or tractor unit, or any one of the applicators in Chapter Five. The electrostatic ionizer will force DE to cling to the undersides of leaves.

MITES

Covered under this topic are bed mites, bird mites, chiggers, clove mites, dust mites, grain mites, harvest mites, house mites, itch mites, lice, mold mites, scabies, straw itch mites, tropical rat mites, and other household pests.

Keep the immune system strong and healthy to help avoid susceptibility to mites. Just as for fleas and lice, it is vital to treat everyone and all animals and birds that share the same space, at the same time. Lightly sprinkle DE in carpets, cracks, baseboards, pet bedding, under furniture and couch cushions, in closets and cupboards, and on doormats and patios. Leave for 2 to 4 days, then vacuum. For severe cases reapply every 10 days to prevent re-hatching and re-infesting, as eggs hatch 10 days to 3 weeks after being laid.

Smother bed mites by lightly dusting with DE, and then seal the mattress with plastic covering for 3 to 7 days. Wash all bed linens, clothing and towels in hot water on the longest cycle, then dry in the drier. Sprinkle soft toys with DE and seal in an air-tight plastic bag for 3 to 7 days, then place in the drier for a half hour.

See Resources for informative websites about mites.

See also Spider Mites below.

MOTHS

(See Grain Weevils—Chapter Three, and Silverfish below).

PET FOOD BUGS

Pure food grade DE is harmless to animals, birds and soil: The government has approved of food grade DE specifically for use in animal feed, and grain and seed storage. **Caution:** Do not use industrial, or swimming pool or aquarium filter DE as it's extremely hazardous for this purpose. Look for these terms on all DE labels for use in or around food: **Anti-Caking Agent,** Amorphous Silicon Dioxide (at least 86 percent or higher with 0.1 percent crystalline silica or less), or **Grain Storage Protectant.** These DE products should not have any other additive, neither synthetic chemical, nor natural unnamed *inert* ingredient. However, mineral oxides are fine, which are the original natural trace minerals found inherently in DE (asides from the predominant mineral silicon dioxide).

Dried pet food treated with DE: Ants, weevils, beetles, and flies are notorious hitchhikers. When bringing dried pet food into the home, first dump it all into a plastic trashcan and thoroughly mix 1-oz. (8 level teaspoons) of plain food grade DE to every pound of dry pet food. Best keep grains stored in an airtight container. DE is a natural deodorizer and will help keep flies away from food when left out for pets. *(See also Grains, Chapter Three).*

Pet parasites: Many veterinarians are advocates of DE and use it to treat and kill internal parasites. Some animal owners sprinkle a teaspoon of food grade DE on the pet's daily food. DE will stimulate digestion and add 14 trace minerals to benefit the animal's health, which may result in a shiny coat and eyes, as well as increased energy levels and alertness. Do not be concerned if some of the pure food grade DE gets on your pet's fur or paws, which they might lick and ingest. The DE will continue to kill internal parasites on the way through the digestive tract. Discuss this with your veterinarian.

(See also the anecdotal user comments in Chapter Four for ideas on how others successfully treated their pets or animals by adding DE to their food).

SCALE

These small sucking wingless insects have a hard scaly covering. They attach to plants and trees and can cause substantial damage. Signs to look out for include: scales causing poor growth, pale dehydrated leaves, and small fruit that dries out and drops off. The brownish raised spots on an infected plant are actually the insect's shell covering. Apply DE with any of the tools including an electrostatic sprayer (in *Chapter Five*) for best results and to ensure the dust clings to the undersides of leaves and twigs where scales dine. Repeat after rain and as necessary to kill both the female scales and their eggs.

SILVERFISH

To eliminate silverfish in paper products, books and damp dark closets: First treat the cause of dampness that attracts silverfish. Dust the bookbindings with DE powder where silverfish are feeding on the binding glue, as they will eventually destroy it. Diatomaceous Earth is a colorless, odorless and stainless powder that helps absorb moisture, acts as a deodorizer and natural insecticide, and won't harm paper. Use a shaker jar with holes in the lid, or salt or spice shaker to sprinkle DE on book edges and between pages, folded maps, or pieces of paper or cloth. Use a crack and crevice applicator, or mustard or ketchup bottle to get DE into hard-to-reach places. Put DE behind books, in dark cupboards, and under floor coverings. DE may be left in place, undisturbed, if not visibly obtrusive.

SLUGS AND SNAILS

How to make a snail sneeze: Sprinkle DE powder using a kitchen colander or flour sieve, or spray DE liquid solution (Chapter Five) on snail trails, the soil near plants, under hideouts such as slats of wood, mulch and debris, and around potted plants. Repeat if DE gets washed away after rain or watering. To make a snail barrier that acts as a repellant to fence snails out, spread DE ¼-inch deep in a 2-inch wide band around any area for protection. For best results, the DE should be kept dry, but if it gets wet, it will continue working after drying as long as it is not washed away.

SOW OR PILL BUGS

To stop root and stem damage: Keep garden debris cleaned up where these bugs like to hide and feed on decaying organic matter. Remove decomposing vegetation, boards, rocks or old mulch. Sprinkle a light coating of DE with a colander over troublesome areas. Reapply DE if water washes it away. Apply fresh coarse mulch. Water early in the morning so the DE, mulch and plants can dry during the day.

SPIDER MITES

Using a hose-end sprayer, apply a liquid solution of DE. Pay attention to the underside of leaves. Better results may be obtained using an electrostatic nozzle to make DE stick by polarity to the undersides of leaves. *(See Chapter Five for how to make a DE liquid spray and for more information on the electrostatic ionizer).*

TERMITES

Don't invite termites to make their home out of your home: Prevention is the best approach for controlling termites. Colonies consist of a queen, sterile workers and soldiers, who prefer to lunch on homes; some like dry wood and some like it wet. Your best defense is a watchful eye. Check for warning signs at least once a year. What termites leave behind for you to look for is: soft, crumbly, tunneled, hollow-sounding wood. Tap it with a hammer and keep an eye out for fecal pellets and shredded wings. Your local Cooperative Extension Agent will help you distinguish between an ant and a termite, if you can't tell. Best of all, trained beagles of professional exterminators can sniff out an infestation.

Get rid of the termite's favorite haunting places. They are attracted to water, so remove and repair sources of moisture: seal up leaks and cracks, clean up relocated drains and construction debris and install sump pumps. Above ground, dry-wood termites will seek out cracks in the outer shell of the house, so seal them out. A termite's front door entry will often be through your attic.

New homebuilders can use DE in the early stages of construction. Be sure that outside buildings are off the ground and on concrete blocks. Use non-toxic biologically preserved wood or treat it yourself. Before the vapor barrier is laid down, apply a generous amount of DE to the bare soil, paying particular attention along the footing. Blow a dry layer of Diatomaceous Earth (DE) beneath buildings and on foundations with a leaf blower. Once the foundation is poured and set, apply more DE along the outside perimeter where the wall joists will be laid down. This will eliminate excess moisture and discourage pests from making your home their own. Blow DE into the wall voids. (To apply DE to large areas, see *Chapter Five—Tools and Applicators*).

Wear a dust mask and eye goggles while using a bulb duster to blow a thin layer of DE onto exposed wood. Find out from your Cooperative Extension Agent when swarming season is and blast away just before those termites hunt out your house. Use a dry powder commercial spray applicator, or hire an Integrative Pest Management (IPM) consultant to spread 100 percent plain DE over and under insulation in the attic. This application will not only create a barrier against termites, but will kill any other bug that comes in contact with it, including spiders and scorpions that frequent attics and basements. As long as DE stays dry and remains there, it does not break down or become ineffective. It will still be lying in wait for the next season's attack but it pays to check on it.

WASPS

Use a liquid DE spray: Wearing goggles, a mask and protective clothing if necessary, spray the nest and hovering wasps with DE. Keep as far away as possible from angry wasps *(See Chapter Five for the liquid DE recipe and application methods)*.

Anecdotal User Testimonials:
How DE Protects The Home & Garden

(Sharing the successful testimonies of others may help expand your own experiences and success with DE).

Safe use of DE at a mobile home park: "As the property manager of a mobile home park in Tucson, Arizona, where we have been using DE for eight months, we are thrilled with excellent results. Nothing we tried previously seemed to work for ants, but now

DE has done it so far for us. We just dust DE on the ant hills as well as a 12 or 14-inch circle around them. Things are pretty well under control inside of two hours. Cockroaches and crickets are controlled by dusting under the mobile homes and down the sewer connections. Here again, control is quite rapid and lasting. Best of all we can assure our tenants that the material we are using is safe for themselves, their children and pets."

DE won against cockroaches but chemicals failed: "We are plagued in the summer with hordes of loathsome outdoor cockroaches that multiply like mad under some old lumber in our yard. Only a few were exterminated with malathion and diazinon spray but fresh batches kept coming on and on, so we switched to DE. Were we surprised? Within three weeks all the cockroaches were gone, completely gone."

DE gives roses a break from aphids: "I noticed an infestation of aphids on two miniature roses, so I got out the duster bottle and doused all 50 of my minis. I dusted again about a month later. Then in one week I was out again with the duster, but there were no signs of aphids. I'm not sure this was a fair test, but I'm convinced now this organic pesticide has unlimited potential."

DE passes test for brown dog tick: The USDA Livestock Division tested DE on the brown dog tick and rated it 100 percent effective. "Any animal treated with this product will be a happy, healthy animal. It can also be used to treat the sleeping area of the animal inside and out, including the house rug."

Frisky flea free puppies: "My son was given a litter of beautiful Chocolate Lab pups because they were so infested with fleas. He used food grade DE, and on the first day the dogs and their bedding areas were suddenly free of fleas. The puppies were in good shape when he took them to the vet a few days later. He also used it in their feed. They are now beautiful, happy, healthy puppies."

3

Diatomaceous Earth (DE) For Use in Grain & Seed Storage

Important Caution:

In accordance with the officially recommended 1997 OSHA safety standard, all tips in this chapter suggest using only food grade Diatomaceous Earth, which is pure amorphous "non-crystalline" silicon dioxide, with 0.1 percent ($1/10$th of 1 percent) or less "crystalline" silica and no additives.

Food Grade
Diatomaceous Earth Is Also Known As:

* Grain Storage Protectant

* Animal Feed Additive

* Anti-Caking Agent

* Inert Carrier

Practical Tips For Preventing Weevils In Grains

Diatomaceous Earth is approved by the United States Department of Agriculture (USDA) as an *Anti-Caking Agent* for use in animal feed. Diatomaceous Earth is also approved for internal and external use by the Food and Drug Administration (FDA) and is controlled by Food Codex ratings.

The use of Diatomaceous Earth in food is not new. In fact DE has an ancient history of use in agriculture and grain storage. The Chinese have been adding DE to their grain and animal feed for 4,000 years. DE was also found in the Egyptian pyramids protecting grain from deterioration by moisture, mold and insects, and various countries in Europe and Asia have been using DE mainly since the early 1900's.

The use of DE in grain for animals: The agricultural industry uses DE for improving and protecting animal feed grains. DE is also used to protect nuts, beans, legumes and rice. Farmers, veterinarians and kennel owners have long used DE in animal feed for horses, cows, ranch cattle, poultry, ostriches, pigs and dogs, etc. Aside from the benefit of DE as a safe and natural insecticide against grain weevils, DE also aids in nutrition by acting to separate the particles of animal feed and grains, thereby preventing "clumping," and also making the feed less likely to mold by removing moisture. Farmers like to use DE as it improves flowability, mixability, and handling. When DE is ingested by the animal it is exposed to both bacterial and enzymatic processes. DE increases digestibility of the feed or grain, and provides 14 trace minerals for improving and maintaining animal health.

The use of DE in grain for human consumption: In the USA, the government has allowed granaries and seed mills to use DE in grain and seed storage which is intended for ingestion by humans, animals or poultry. Some granaries and mills use DE not only to keep grain free of bugs, but also in the processing stage, and to keep it dry to prevent disintegration during transportation and in storage before the food reaches supermarket shelves. For success, grains should be cleaned and treated right after harvest, although insect eggs which already existed may be present for a period of time after treatment before dying of dehydration. Whole grains can be rinsed in a strainer before cooking to remove the DE. (See *"Anecdotal Comments"* below).

Good housekeeping comes first: Firstly, avoid attracting moths that contaminate grain and flour with their larvae. Remove the food haven and block their source of allurement. Transfer all grains and flours to airtight, rubber-sealed jars, or plastic containers, but be sure to seal the lids correctly to do any good. After thoroughly cleaning up any spilled grain, including that which gets on the outside of the container itself, lightly sprinkle pure 100 percent food grade DE *(Grain Storage Protectant)* on the shelves between containers, getting DE into all crevices. Leave for at least 24 to 48 hours before wiping up, or leave DE in place indefinitely to continually act as a repellant.

What to do with grain already infested with weevils and larvae? Before storing foods just brought home from the supermarket, check all fresh grocery items such as flour, cereals, nuts, seeds and whole grains. If a product is already infested with eggs, insect shells, dead moths or silk webs, it is not worth keeping and further risking contamination of other stored grains.

Put the infested product in an airtight container such as a plastic bowl with a tight fitting lid and freeze for one week to kill the remaining insects and larvae. Then carefully dispose of the infested food in the garbage in a sealed plastic bag. Check pantry shelves for signs of larvae and silk webs. If any are found, empty shelves and wash containers with hot soapy water. Wipe off unwashable containers, rinsing the cloth in hot soapy water after to avoid spreading contamination. Cover shelves with a fine sprinkling of DE, then place cleaned containers back on top until all signs of weevils and larvae are gone.

Telltale signs of bugs in grains: Moth and beetle larvae are small worms that look a bit like your grains of rice. They dine on pantry grains, flours, legumes, seeds, nuts, etc. That's where they go to lay their larvae, which feed, pupate and hatch into adults that look to your food to lay more eggs—a pesky cycle. In the process, these pests will leave signs of their presence: skins left behind, cast off cocoons, telltale tiny holes in your packages of rice, oats, flours, etc., and silk webs inside the lids of containers and between the grains.

How To Protect Flours, Grains, Nuts And Seeds From Bugs In Containers Of: 1-Lb, 1-Quart, 25-100 Lb, And 1-Ton

How to protect ground flours from weevils with DE: According to Dr Subramanyam PhD, who researched DE for use in whole grains, etc., at the University of Minnesota, food grade DE can be safely added to ground flour at the rate of 1-oz of DE to every 1-lb of flour. Thoroughly mix for even distribution. Obviously there is no way to wash DE out of ground flour. However, it should be food grade and does add 14 beneficial trace minerals. Chances are, since almost everyone has eaten flour before, we have been unknowingly ingesting DE which was added during the milling process and warehouse storage.

How to protect 1-lb and 1-quart storage jars of whole grains, seeds, nuts, legumes and rice with DE: To fill a 1-lb container, measure the grain then empty into a bowl. Add ½-teaspoon of food grade Diatomaceous Earth labeled as (*Grain Storage Protectant*) and mix well. Return grain to the container and close tightly. Shake well to ensure even distribution of DE throughout. If not using for some time, use a salt or spice shaker filled with DE to sprinkle a thin layer on the top of the grain. To protect a 1-quart storage jar, pour grains into a large bowl, and then add 1-teaspoon of DE. Mix well and store as above.

DE registered and labeled as Grain Storage Protectant is 100 percent food grade Diatomaceous Earth (with no additives) and is not hazardous to health. Food grade DE does not harm if left in the cooking, however most prefer to wash off any dirt and even insect remains before cooking.

How to protect a 25-pound container of grain with DE:

Apply 1-cupful of DE to each 25-pound sack of grain to be treated. A pail or any other container can be used for thorough mixing as follows: sprinkle a coating of DE into the base of the container then add a 3-inch deep layer of grain. Using a flour sieve or colander, sprinkle a light coating of DE over the grain. Repeat the layering process until the container is almost filled with grain. Place the lid on tightly then roll or shake the container until the powder is thoroughly mixed, and a very light coating covers each kernel. Pour treated grain into a dry container for storage. Sprinkle DE on the top surface of grain. Do not mix the final top layer of DE. Seal well.

Flour sacks may be used, but ensure that the outsides of each one are given a light dusting of DE using a flour sieve, colander or coffee can with holes punched in the lid. Repeat as necessary if bags are moved which would disturb or remove some of the insecticide. An airtight seal will help prevent moisture in the grain. When kept in this condition in a cool dry storage area, grains can last for many years. To wash DE off the grain before cooking, place in a colander and wash with running tap water.

How to protect 100-pounds of grain with DE: To mix DE throughout, apply in layers as above. A 100-pound sack can be top-dressed with as little as ½-ounce of DE. Sprinkle a layer of DE with a flour sieve or colander over the top layer of grain before tightly sealing. Sprinkle DE on the outside and also on top of the container.

How to protect 1-ton of grain with DE: DE is applied usually at the bottom of the elevator leg, at the required rate for the particular grain. This is best done with a variable rate screw feeder from a hopper device.

Treat the bottom 10 percent layer of the grain with 1-pound of DE per 35-bushels, or 1-pound per ton.

Treat newly harvested grain immediately at the time of entry before storage. In this way, the cost of treating grain or seed is most economical and can result in substantial savings to users over other types of controls and fumigants.

The amount of DE required varies with cleanliness of the grain or seed to be stored. Clean grain or seed of course requires lesser application of DE than grain or seed containing a lot of dust and chaff that interferes with the protectant action. Dust and chaff having some absorbent ability may absorb practically an equal weight of the DE so allowance for applying more DE must be made for this factor. The best remedy is to clean the grain first.

If the grain is protected somewhere within the hatching range of insects, egg infestation will be killed in either larval or adult stages (usually the larval).

Mixing DE throughout 1-ton of grain: Using hoppers and rate dispensers, apply 7-pounds of DE powder directly onto each 1-ton of clean dry grain, beans, legumes, nuts or seeds to be treated. Mix thoroughly, coating every grain and store as above. The success of storing grain or seed rests on lightly coating the outside surface of each kernel. DE needs to be applied only once as long as it remains undisturbed.

Top dressing only: For surface treating, top-dress with DE at the rate of 4-lbs per 1,000 square feet, or apply 1-lb on the surface layer of each 1-ton. Rake into the top four inches of grain. Then reapply a second dusting to the surface where it should remain undisturbed. This will not however protect grain that is already infested throughout.

Applying DE with screw feeders: Apply the DE to bulk grain as it is placed in storage by means of an inexpensive adjustable screw feeder. The DE is fed evenly by the screw feeder through an elevator leg, then mixed evenly with the grain as it travels to storage, either on a belt or in a screw conveyor. Plastic tubing can be used for delivery of the dust should the arrangement of facilities not permit the feeder to be placed adjacent to the grain conveyor. Set up screw feeder to deposit DE into the elevator leg, belt or auger-type conveyor where it is convenient to service or refill the feeder. The screw feeder must be properly dispensing DE into the elevator leg or conveyor at all times when the grain is moving.

It is important to know the rate (tons per hour) the grain is being moved. By weighing DE and adjusting the feeder on 2-5 minute runs, you can set the screw feeder to the required 7-pounds per ton ratio. Generally, it is best to put DE into the grain at a point where it will travel the farthest and mix the most before the grain reaches storage.

Permanent protection from insects is secured by proper and thorough mixing of DE with the grain. It is of utmost importance that each kernel has a light coating of DE powder. Following these simple and logical methods will give assurance of obtaining the maximum results in grain storage.

Other Tips To Insect-Proof Grain Warehouses And Bins

- To control Indian meal moth and anguomois moths, use DE in all food handling and grain storage areas, such as flour mills, warehouses, and food processing plants.

- First, keep good housekeeping practices in the warehouse. To avoid creating an insect sanctuary, clean all debris from empty bins, truck beds, box cars, and ship holds, then treat with DE when emptied and again before loading.

- The most effective method of application is with an electrostatic duster which delivers an ionized charge helping the dust to stick by polarity to ceilings, walls, and around and inside processing equipment, conveyor belts, etc. Crack and crevice nozzles are also available. *(See Chapter Five for Application Tools and information on electrostatic ionizers).*

- To prevent migration of insects pay special attention to sealing and treating cracks, joints, crevices and corners in and around the facility where insects crawl and hide. It is best to treat again during early spring and warmer months when insects are actively emerging from their hiding places.

- Treat the aeration system of the building to kill insects crawling or flying in from outside.

- Remove grain residues from combine headers, augers, conveyer belts, elevators, grain transporting vehicles or containers, and dust DE on all these surfaces that come in contact with the grain before harvest.

- Properly set the combine header to minimize kernel breakage during harvesting.

- Clean grain before storage.

- Do not mix fresh grain with old or infested grain.

- Avoid breathing airborne dust when applying DE. Wear a mask and goggles.

- Pre-treat using DE on the inside of all containers or any other surface that will touch the grain using either a hand held power duster, back-pack unit, sandblasting gun, aeration fan, or electrostatic ionizer. Approximately 1-lb of DE per 1,000 square-feet is recommended on all interior wall surfaces of empty storage areas.

- An empty bin can be treated in less than a minute after cleaning with a sandblasting gun. The pressure of the compressed air inlet into the sandblasting gun must be at least 100 psi.

- It is recommended that any empty area be treated and left undisturbed for two or three days to eliminate existing infestations before filling.

- Maintain weed-free surrounding fields to cut down on seeds mixing with the grain.

- Treat a six-foot radius around the storage facility and outside foundations. Repeat after each rainfall.

- DE kills all stored grain insects (such as weevils, beetles, moths, and borers) within 2 to 14 days after making contact.

- Dust over lightly again (including the walls) after the container is loaded.

- With the first appearance of moths, apply DE at monthly intervals. In severe infestations, break up webbing with a rake before dusting, and make a second application within two weeks.

- It is desirable to re-dust immediately each time the storage area is emptied and cleaned.

- Pay attention to metal grain bins with perforated floors, which allow broken grains and dust to sift through and collect onto the sub-floor (plenum). When possible, remove the perforated floors to clean the plenum area. Always leave a layer of DE on the sub-floor (plenum) once it is cleaned.

- Don't overlook grain or feed accumulations in empty feed sacks, dusts created by feed grinders, seed litter from hay-mowers, and grain-based rodenticides.

- Treat areas around animal self-feeders, and where seed live-stock feed and pet food is stored.

- Keep stored grain as far away as possible from feed rooms and bins.

- Grain held in the range of 12 to 14 percent moisture can be stored for a minimum of 6 to 12 months.

What To Look For On DE Grain Labels

When looking for the correct type of DE for protecting grains against bugs, be sure the label states **Grain Storage Protectant,** or **Anti-Caking Agent.** It should be pure 100 percent food grade Diatomaceous Earth with no other additives such as pyrethrum or PBO, and have 0.1 percent ($^1/_{10th}$ of 1 percent) or less *crystalline* silica.

You will not find the word "safe" on DE animal feed additive labels in USA—even if DE is intended for animal feed and grain storage and has been certified or designated as GRAS *(Generally Recognized As Safe)* by the government *(Federal Register 1961)*—currently, this terminology cannot be applied by law to labels. Nor can the label state "non-poisonous" when added to cereals and grains for storage if intended for human consumption. As an *Animal Feed Additive*, it's required by regulation, the amount of DE added for storage is not to exceed 2 percent of the total weight of the animal food ration.

Anecdotal User Testimonials:
How DE Protects Grains And Seeds

The WHO gives thumbs-up to DE in grain: The World Health Organization and the Food and Agriculture Organization, both arms of the UN, were pleased with test results conducted in Africa. It is believed that DE has real value in third world countries, where protection of stored grain against insects is an enormous problem. When DE is added to grains for third world countries, over 50 percent is saved from loss by insects, mold and moisture.

Seed test succeeded for state agency: A Kansas agricultural experimental project was conducted to determine the effectiveness of DE in preventing damage to sunflower seeds by the Indian meal moth. DE was reported to have a significant improvement over other controls. In addition, rodent hairs, insect fragments and fecal matter in the seeds were significantly reduced.

Seed labs approval of DE: The Agricultural Seed Laboratories of Phoenix, Arizona, conducted *A Study to Determine the Effect of Insecticide on the Germination of Grain, Sorghum, Barley and Wheat Planting Seed.* Their conclusions were most enlightening: "The germination results of all samples were within the allowable tolerance of each other, even when excessive amount of DE was used. Seed of low viability showed no adverse effect."

DE keeps the sweetest smelling grain with the least bug parts: Hayden Flour Mills in Tempe, Arizona, was one of the state's largest grain storage businesses. Irv Manly, who was superintendent of Hayden Mills at one time, remembers the day that a guy named de Lisle arrived with his strange dust DE. "I didn't see how it could possibly work, but we were having some trouble with our other fumigants, so I said, 'All right, let's give it a try'. Well, I never saw anything like it in my life. We never had another problem with insects after using nothing but Diatomaceous Earth for the last 15 years, until new owners bought the mill and went back to chemicals. With DE, we had our dead insect fragments down to 1 part per thousand (ppt) and there isn't an elevator in the country that ever gets below 15 ppt. When you walked into other elevators, all you ever smelled was chemicals. But when you walked into our elevator, you smelled grain." The success at Hayden Mills using DE helped prompt the United States Department of Agriculture (USDA) to conduct its own investigation of the effects of Diatomaceous Earth on stored grain.

Grain treated with DE gets a long life: The former superintendent of Hayden Mills Granary says, "After a few months of experimentation, we got completely away from the use of chemicals. There was no need to subject our customers, or our employees to possible contamination, especially when the DE performed even better. When Senator Carl Hayden, owner of the Mill died, the organization was sold. The new people would not even listen to the use of a non-chemical product as an insecticide. Not wanting to be involved again in the use of chemicals, I decided it was time for me to retire. It was a terrible disappointment for me to see a poison-free elevator be recontaminated so unnecessarily."

Before the superintendent's retirement he stated, "I have probably 200 or 300 pages of reports, mainly from Kansas State University, in conjunction with the Department of Agriculture, where they ran test after test on Diatomaceous Earth protecting grain. I have a sample of grain that was put up in 1976, having been treated one time only with DE. That grain is as fresh and clean as it can be."

"Hayden executives at that time were so impressed by the results obtained from treating a small elevator that they decided to risk $¾ million worth of grain to do an all-out test. Again, the results were superlative."

Infested dog pellets made good again with DE: The former superintendent of Hayden Mills Granary, Arizona, stated, "We bought a carload of dog food that was badly infested. The local purchaser refused the shipment and it was offered to us. With no previous experience, we decided to take a chance. We carefully opened each bag so they could be reused. Using plenty of DE, we put the mixture in a silo for two weeks, ran the pellets through a cleansing process, re-bagged it and delivered the load to the same people who turned it down before."

Bad grain losses hugely reduced—big dollar savings with DE: A superintendent of a Tohoka, Texas, grain elevator states, "We treated 36 cars of milo with DE. Close and regular inspections were made of this grain by both our personnel and Commodity Credit personnel. The milo was continuously found to be completely free of all live weevils. Only dead weevils were found. Previously, we had been forced to ship away seven million pounds of untreated grain in one year due to insect damage. However, the DE treated grain was kept in storage because there just wasn't any damage. As any superintendent knows, the cost of moving infected grain is tremendous. Therefore, this meant a great saving to us—this treated grain could be retained in storage with complete confidence that it would remain in excellent condition."

4

Diatomaceous Earth (DE) For Agricultural Uses

---

* ANIMAL & BIRD FARMS
* CROPS & ORCHARDS
* PETS

Important Caution:

In accordance with the officially recommended 1997 OSHA safety standard, all tips in this chapter suggest using only food grade Diatomaceous Earth, which is pure amorphous "non-crystalline" silicon dioxide, with 0.1 percent ($^1/_{10th}$ of 1 percent) or less "crystal-line" silica and no additives.

Food Grade
Diatomaceous Earth is Also known as:

** Grain Storage Protectant*

** Animal Feed Additive*

** Anti-Caking Agent*

** Inert Carrier*

1) Diatomaceous Earth (DE) For Use On Animal Farms

Advantages to animal farmers using DE: In USA the government has allowed DE for agricultural use since the 1960's. Veterinarians and farmers have been using DE for at least a half century as a safe and natural trace mineral supplement, insecticide and anti-parasitic (wormer) for livestock, birds and pets. Naturally all these uses of DE result in improved animal health and growth, increased profits, less worry and work, and happier farmers.

Less chemicals, losses, odors, bugs and flies using DE: The use of 100 percent food grade natural DE on farms helps keep milk safe, pure and free of toxic chemicals. It is used to control a multitude of pests around barns, stables, milking parlors, fodders, exercise and holding areas, and directly on the animals. DE helps prevent animal feed from clumping and molding, while it improves handling and flowability. DE is also used at county fairs and horse shows as a non-toxic method of controlling flies, fleas, and lice. Being a natural deodorizer, DE also controls manure smells and moisture, resulting in far fewer flies. DE also helps prevent damage and loss of dried animal feed in storage due to insect infestation, moisture, and mold—a loss that can be surprisingly large to the farmer and costly to replace.

How to eliminate animal parasites using DE: When animals ingest feed containing DE it immediately begins to clear the system of health destroying intestinal parasites. Farmers may begin to notice the lessening of scours (diarrhea) within a couple days. Offering DE for a minimum of 60 days is suggested at 2 percent of the dry weight of grain ration fed on a free-choice basis. For effective use, DE must be fed long enough to affect, kill and eliminate any newly hatching eggs, or cycling of the parasites through the lungs and back to the stomach. DE's anti-parasitic effect on animals is simple, gentle and natural, causing no toxic shock to the animal. Some other health benefits which will take a few days to weeks, or even months to become apparent are: weight gain, better growth, stamina, and shiny coats and eyes.

Why DE is nutritional for animals: The trillions of aquatic diatoms of which DE is comprised, once flourished as algae plants and has been affectionately called the "meadow grass of the sea." Uncountable fish and other marine creatures thrived on this rich aquatic food source. Millions of years ago when those diatoms died, they dropped to the bottom of the ocean or lake, forming a soft rock deposit, holding within a vast nutritional treasure. Modern mining, milling and packaging, enables these rich aquatic trace minerals to be transported and re-packaged for animal, bird and human use, in the same way as the nutrients in grass are packaged when cut and dried for hay. Extensive tests by the University of Arizona have proven that the presence of DE on any grain used for animal feed makes for far better fodder due to the presence of at least 14 trace minerals. When this DE supplement is ingested it improves the well-being of livestock in multiple ways.

Nutrition Benefits Of DE Trace Minerals In Animal Feed

- Improves and stimulates metabolism and digestion. Doing a protein analysis on the manure can prove this point. Animals fed DE absorb a larger percentage of protein from their regular diet.

- Improves appetite.

- Stops dirt licking and corral gnawing (which is caused by an animal's effort to get more trace minerals).

- Increases stamina by building up the blood cells, tissues and bones.

- Allows greater weight gain for less feed consumption.

- Absorbs destructive and poisonous sediments in the intestinal tract.

- Saves the albumen in the stomach and guards against destructive harmful acids.

- Improves the general health of the animal and puts a noticeable sheen on the coat and sparkle in the eye. Young or sick animals not only put on weight, but grow faster and thrive better.

- DE does not cause an accumulation of poisonous synthetic chemical residues in the bodies of warm-blooded animals, therefore leaving milk and cream pure and uncontaminated.

- Increases milk production.

- Improves animal contentedness, disposition and reduces stress.

- Acts as an intestinal tract cleanser and detoxifier. Helps prevent impaction and rids the colon of parasites.

Analysis Of The Minerals In DE And How Animals Benefit

Note: The following is an approximation. Each brand of DE varies, according to the location of the mine, history of ancient activity, and types of diatom. Three of the elements below are of a rare earth group—gallium, titanium and vanadium. Research indicates these rare earth elements are very important for both animal and plant nutrition.

Silicon Dioxide: 86.2 percent and above is especially effective for bone and hair growth. Actually, silicon dioxide is a major mineral not a trace (minor) mineral.

Calcium: 5 percent (and above) strengthens bones, aids in growth.

Magnesium: 0.3 percent (and above) strengthens bones, aids in growth.

Titanium Dioxide: 2.0 percent keeps the animal's coat clean and shiny.

Gallium: 002 percent increases the effectiveness of the stomach and strengthens bone structure.

Vanadium: 002 percent acts as a catalyst for calcium in the digestive tract especially during and immediately after pregnancy. When not present in dairy cattle they are more susceptible to milk fever.

Strontium: 01 percent governs sulfates in the digestive tract of cattle.

Sodium: 1.0 percent acts as an internal cleansing agent.

Boron: 0.6 percent acts as a germicide and necessary for bone growth.

Conclusion: All of these elements are so perfectly enjoined by nature that they appear to work in unison with each other, rather than as individual elements. Thinking of them as individual elements is quite misleading.

Anecdotal User Testimonials:
How DE Protects Animals And Farms

DE improved animal health: "Our animals simply thrive better, gain weight and are more contented. Our milk production has gone up and vet bills have gone down. It's the greatest thing going for farmers. It may be the only thing we can use that would be totally safe as both an insecticide and a feed supplement to supply the nutrition they need for growth and development."

Animal feed bags have no bugs: "I've had a problem of bringing bugs home from the feed store on the feed bags. Now to eliminate this pesky nuisance, as we unload and stack the bags, we sprinkle them with DE, which kills the bugs on the bags."

Fly larvae on farm doesn't survive DE: "We are feeding and dusting the coats of our dairy goats, llamas, sheep, a donkey and a horse with DE. After cleanup we dust the barn and pens (daily) with DE using a hand-pump sprayer. The wet spots get an extra handful of DE after raking. Before we started using DE the raking turned up a host of fly larvae. This year with the DE there are practically no larvae. There are probably about as many flies around our farmhouse now as you would find around a city house. Certainly, there are not enough flies to ruin an occasional barbecue or a lot of evening porch swinging. We highly recommend DE."

No organ damage found in animals fed DE: A study at the laboratory division of the Department of Agriculture, Michigan, found no evidence of organ abnormalities in dairy cows having free-choice access to food grade DE for approximately five years. The animal pathologist examined the vital organs and intestinal components both macroscopically and microscopically which were submitted under affidavit. These components consisted of brain, thyroid, rib section, lung, heart, liver, true stomach, small intestine section, large intestine section, pancreas, kidney, bladder and forestomach.

No toxic residues in meat and milk when DE is added to animal food grain: The head of the Department of Veterinary Medicine at the University of Illinois, reported, "I can relate our experiences with DE when it was incorporated as 2 percent ration fed to cattle. It had no apparent adverse effects and there was no evidence that any of it was absorbed into the meat, and no residues appeared in the milk. In toxicity tests using FDA protocol there is no damage even when the animals are fed in much larger quantities. One outstanding benefit of feeding animals food grade Diatomaceous Earth is that they seem to produce manures with a certain degree of built-in fly control and reduced odor."

Milk and butterfat go up while flies, larvae, gnawing corrals and warbles disappear: A dairyman states, "It's good to see Diatomaceous Earth available to dairymen. As someone who has used it for over thirty years I know it works. We began feeding food grade DE free-choice to our herd of purebred Jerseys. Within a few days the cows completely stopped licking the soil and making holes in the corrals. DE seemed to have an element the cows needed that several of the other types of minerals we tried previously didn't have."

He continues, "After feeding DE continuously at 3-oz. per day per cow, we found the production of milk and butterfat increased by an average of 15 percent per cow."

A pleasant surprise and peculiarity we observed was the lack of flies. We did a test on the effectiveness of DE upon the fly population. Our first pen of heifers had no DE in their feed. There was a multitude of fly larvae in a shovel full of manure. The second pen of heifers had been fed DE. There was only one larvae in a shovel full of manure dug in similar conditions. Also our warbles problem came to an abrupt halt after we started feeding DE to the cows."

Cows rather partial to DE: When a dairy sanitation inspector noticed a cow lazily licking up DE he said, "I wouldn't have believed it if I hadn't seen it. She acts as if she likes it.

At first, a motor applicator and a white cloud of DE dust will frighten some animals, but after a few dustings the animals know they won't be hurt. Within a couple weeks most animals appreciate the treatment so much that they come right up to the applicator for dusting because they realize they are going to get relief."

A dairy farmer had trouble with the city over flies and manure odor. He started using DE, applying it with a backpack ionizer that dramatically reduced the flies. He said, "I had the pleasure of seeing a large herd of cows immediately trot to the fence for their application of DE." After dusting the cows with DE and also feeding it to them, the farmer got rid of both his odor troubles with the city and the bothersome flies. Now he feeds DE free-choice. Each cow ate an average of 4-oz. per day within two weeks of starting the DE feeding.

DE boosts animal growth: A horse trainer who fed DE to his horses said, "I saw a tremendous improvement in the rate of growth of our young horses, while no other dietary changes were made when feeding except the addition of DE."

Glowing dairy animal health and no vet bills: A dairy farmer states, "We feed our cows 2-heaped tablespoonfuls each of DE per day as that seems to be the amount the cows will clean up. Their health has improved greatly with better coats and they no longer eat dirt, nor do they have internal parasites that would cause loss of production or need doctoring. One of the most noticeable differences has been in the lack of vet bills. Now, warbles are non-existent and there are only about $1/5$ of the flies. Some of the people from the Health Department have commented on the scarcity of odors and flies on our place. We are real pleased with the results we are getting from DE."

Goodbye to warbles & bad odor: "All our cows were just loaded with grubs or warbles on their backs. After feeding the DE for about three weeks, the grubs started to shrink and disappear completely. Their hair is so shiny and eyes bright. Our bull and young heifers which have not had any DE are still loaded with grubs and they don't have the slick shiny coat. I'd never believe manure could be without foul odor, but our cows that are fed DE have no bad odor."

Cows get too much of a good thing: "Our cows weren't eating the DE very well as we were giving them too much, so we reduced it to $1/2$-cup per cow, once a day. After two or three days the cows really started to like it. They would lick the bottom of the grain box clean."

Drier mangers & no mastitis with DE: "Since feeding the cows 5 to 6 oz. of DE daily our butterfat tests have increased in 5 weeks from 3.7 to 3.9. Mastitis is at a standstill and the manure is drier, which makes sweeping the mangers easier."

No yellow mucus after calving with DE: "After calving we used to have an occasional cow which had to be treated by a veterinarian for yellow mucus. Since using DE we have not run into this trouble."

Flies no longer bug showgrounds: The Arizona National showgrounds in 1989 stated after using DE, "We had another great show without all the pesky flies. We haven't had a problem with flies for three years. That is amazing with all the animals which we have on the grounds during the show."

Sick, starved horses bounce back when fed DE: "Our 4-H Club rescued 25 mistreated and starved miniature horses. As an experienced horsewoman, it was without a doubt the worst case of neglect I'd ever seen. They were a pretty sad lot with an overwhelming amount of lice and parasites. After dusting the horses with DE, the external parasites including the lice just turned to dust. It was great! We also have been adding the DE to their feed for better nutrient absorption. Considering the horses were so terribly underfed at the start, we are now seeing marvelous results on their rib covering and the quality of their coats."

Lab confirms no parasites after horses are fed DE: A horse owner stated that his horses had not been wormed for one year. After three months of feeding DE, Edmar Medical Laboratories made a feces test. Results: "No parasites or ova noted."

Horses almost die of scours until given DE: A horse trainer from Florida stated, "I have seen this product work a miracle on two of our walking horses. They were about to die due to scours, which could not be cleared up by any known medications. As a last resort we added 5-oz. of DE twice daily to the horse feed. I was skeptical at first, but what was there to lose? The horses had been slowly wasting away. I am happy with the outcome. In three days their manure was beginning to firm up and in two more days it was normal, which noticeably reduced the flies. After the horses' internal parasites were treated with the DE, their appetite increased, they gained weight, and had a much healthier appearance. I now refer to this natural mineral feed supplement as a 'miracle product' and I recommend it to other trainers and horsemen."

Glossy horse coats & no colic: "I have been feeding DE to my show horses, race horses, horses in training, stallions, mares and foals. We have seen an improvement in their hair as well as their attitude. We feel the attitude is the result of fewer to no flies in the stalls. The DE present in the fecal matter prohibits the larvae and development of adult flies. The DE also helps prevent impaction, which helps prevent colic."

DE gets rid of worms in colt: "The first benefit I noticed came approximately two weeks after feeding DE to a weaning colt. One afternoon I found dead worms in the feces, which indicated that the DE actually rids animals of worms because there was no other change in the diet."

DE improves horse's mobility: "Our horse limped from arthritis in his left shoulder joint. We put approximately ½-cup of DE per day in his feed. Within ten days we could see a definite improvement in his actions. He seemed to be entirely free of stiffness."

Watching TV while sheep de-worm themselves: A certified organic farmer explains how DE helps keep her 96-acre farm free of chemicals when it comes time to de-worm the sheep. "We first started using DE successfully in the animal feed as a natural de-wormer after finding various other methods of worming unacceptable. Getting up early in the mornings to spend another backbreaking day astride all 100 sheep for drenching is not my cup of tea. All the family does now is relax and watch the news while the ewes happily lick a 50/50 blend of DE and trace mineral salt. Now everyday is worming day, without the work, mess and worry of chemicals."

Fringe tape worm gone in sheep fed DE: A sheep farmer says, "Our old ewes were dying with fringe tape worms in the bile ducts. Within two weeks of using DE the dying stopped. Since that time we have lost only two sheep, but these were not from worms. Our animals have improved so much in appearance and general health that they look better than many sheep half their age, and better than any others in the area. According to a highly respected sheep man, our animals are now entirely free from worms."

Pigs more content on DE: "My 650 hogs no longer root after feeding on DE. This means my hogs get the nourishment and minerals they need in a diet that seems to be completely satisfying their needs. Our son raised pigs for his FFA project. He took two out of a litter of seven and put them in another pen. He fed each of these two pigs 4-oz of DE a day. The rest of the litter and the sow did not have any DE. They kept on rooting and just about tore the whole pen apart. However, these two project pigs stopped rooting and chewing on the trough once they got DE in their diet. Even the bedding straw stayed straight and nice. These two pigs fed on DE grew substantially larger than the rest of the pigs from the same litter."

Anecdotal Dosages Farmers Use To Treat Animals With DE

Offer DE with plenty of extra water to prevent constipation. The daily feed rates are as follows:

- **For dry ground feed:** 1 percent DE per weight of feed ration.

- **For grain:** 5 percent DE per weight of feed ration.

- **Kittens:** ½-teaspoon.

- **Cats:** 1-teaspoon.

- **Puppies:** ½ to 1-teaspoon.

- **Dogs under 35 lbs:** 1-teaspoon.

- **Dogs over 35 lbs:** 1-tablespoon.

- **Dogs over 100 lbs:** 2-tablespoons.

- **Hogs:** 2 percent DE per weight of dry feed ration.

- **Goats & Sheep:** 2 percent DE per weight of feed ration.

- **Cows:** ½-cup DE in feed, or 2 percent DE per weight of dry feed ration.

- **Calf:** ¼-cup DE in feed.

- **Horses:** ½ to 1-cup DE in feed, or 2 percent DE per weight of feed ration.

- **Chickens:** 2 to 5 percent DE per weight of feed ration.

Livestock rid themselves of flies & bugs under burlap bags of DE: "Our livestock dust themselves on tightly woven burlap bags full of DE which we hang in barn doorways,

stalls, over gate entrances, or even from trees. The animals are attracted to the DE and work the bag with their heads until they are covered with powder. The self-dusting repels flies, lice, warbles and other bugs, especially around their faces and wherever the dust covers. Contamination of the milk or feed is not a concern as pure 100 percent food grade DE is non-toxic and not a chemical. In enclosed farm buildings we fog DE with a hand-crank applicator or an electrostatic fogger. Whenever animal manure brings flies, we control them by dusting with DE over the whole area including the railings inside and outside the barn."

Animals more contented with the use of DE: "We apply DE on cows and horses with a hand-held puffer, hand crank, or electric or gasoline applicator once or twice a week. Our animals are less stressed after a successful treatment and produce more milk."

2) Diatomaceous Earth (DE) For Use On Bird Farms:

Anecdotal User Testimonials By Bird Owners

Chickens keep their feathers on & hatch more eggs: "Our chickens were practically eaten up with lice in the summer to such an extent they had lost most of their feathers and almost quit laying. Finally, we made a dusting box where they could go dust in the DE at will. I'm happy to report that they look like a different set of chickens, with most of their feathers grown back and egg production about normal. In the poultry house, we mix it with the litter and have no more ticks or lice. We also put it around and over the roost."

Chickens survive and produce better when fed DE: Texas A & M University, College Station ran a test on feeding DE to laying hens with positive results. "Egg production went up while the death rate and egg breakage went down."

75 percent fewer chickens die on poultry farm using DE: A Californian poultry farm with over 1 million birds ran a successful trial against a control group for 2½ months to test the effectiveness of DE. Sixty pounds of DE was added to each 1½-tons of mixed feed for 8,000 laying hens. The following results were observed:

Less flies around the chicken houses where DE was added to the food. Droppings had a drier consistency with no visible wet spots, which made cleaning of the houses much easier. Approximately 75 percent less deaths occurred in the houses where DE was fed. There was also an increase in egg production.

No lice on ostrich ranch: On this Florida Ostrich Ranch there is no sticking your head in the sand after seeing the benefits of DE observed in their ostriches. The owner boasted, "Our birds had lice. We tried unsuccessfully to treat the problem with several chemical products that were expensive to use and toxic to the birds. Finally we purchased a bag of DE. The ostriches loved the treatment. We threw some of the powder on their backs and the ground. The birds immediately started dusting, working the insecticide powder up under their feathers. We were amazed at how long it remained under their feathers. After a few treatments over several weeks, the lice were completely gone. We now use the DE for a regular maintenance program. DE made us and our ostriches very happy."

DE also helps control many other problems in ostrich ranching such as: parasites and biting gnats, dirt eating, impactions due to dirt eating, and a trace mineral deficiency causing leg rotations and poor eggshell quality.

Ostriches relieved of gnats, lice, ants, ticks and fleas: An ostrich farmer in Alabama stated, "We began using DE insecticide when we had a problem with buffalo gnats biting the birds on their face and neck. I knew of an ostrich that died from gnat bites and I did not want the same fate on my farm. We could not get rid of them by any chemical means. Then we tried DE in the barn, on the birds, and also on the sandy dusting areas where they regularly dust themselves. I was astounded. The very first time I used the DE insecticide the gnats disappeared, never to return. Ordinary stable flies, ants and mites also disappeared. I found that a light dusting about every two to three weeks in the summer keeps the birds and barn free of insects. We have also noticed that the barn area no longer has a stable odor."

The ostrich farmer continues, "The birds like to stick close to me when I'm spreading the powder. They love to have me throw it on their backs and to rub it on their necks. After I throw it on their dusting areas, they sit and dust it on themselves. I know I am over dusting them by throwing it with my hand, but the trust that they show me is worth the extra dust used. I can't believe I am liberally applying a dust that kills pesky insects. I'm entertaining my birds. I'm receiving such great benefits, and best of all, I'm not using toxic chemicals."

He states, "I also use DE insecticide on ant mounds in the ostrich pens and elsewhere on the farm. I have found it very effective in killing ants and they do not reappear in treated nests. That's probably because the product does not dissolve—it stays in the nest, killing any ants that walk through it later. I believe I am getting a buildup effect and someday every inch of my farm will be coated in DE. Ants, flies, lice, fleas and ticks will not find their home here."

"To use DE as a feed additive for the ostriches, we open the bags, pour the feed pellets into a huge plastic bucket and add DE, stirring it to coat the pellets. If we do not use all the feed, we leave the feed in the open bucket and bugs are repelled. In other words, I am using the DE just as it is used by the seed and grain industry to keep insects out of grain. We left a bucket of DE coated feed out in the heat and humidity for about a month. The feed was still nice and crisp and free of bugs. Amazing I would say," he happily concludes.

Fewer odors and bugs in bird manure: "Since we have been using DE feed additive for the ostriches, we have noticed several beneficial effects. The stools are consistently good looking while having fewer odors. Flies usually lay their eggs in feces, but in that which contains DE the flies either can't survive landing on the feces, or the fly larvae are not able to escape contact with the DE. In our barn areas we are now virtually free of flies, gnats, fleas, black flies, love bugs, mosquitoes, mites, etc."

DE saves money and man hours in chick pen: Since touring the Tri-State Fair in Amarillo, Texas, a farmer who tried DE on his own ranch stated, "After purchasing DE and a hand-held blower, I rushed back to my ranch and tried it out on my chick pen—a favorite hangout for New Mexican flies. When the dust cleared out, so did the flies. I began feeding the DE to all my birds: 3-pounds of DE to each 50-pound bag of feed. After six days of using DE, I could really tell the differences in the fly population. The flies had not returned for 3 days. The ants that came in contact with the DE died in just a few minutes. I don't know why this product is not publicized at these events. I could have saved a lot of money and man hours over the years if I had known about DE earlier."

3) Diatomaceous Earth (DE) For Use On Crops & Orchards

Older scientific proof of DE's effectiveness: As a result of years of documented studies, researchers and scientists have proven to the FDA and EPA that this multi-million year old natural insecticide is the most non-polluting and effective solution for the health of our future. As far back as 1931, an early pioneer, Polivka, used Diatomaceous Earth to reduce corn borer. For every day's delay in borer silking, there was a 4 percent reduction in the corn borer population. Then, in 1943, the USDA determined that DE had an 86 percent mortality rate against pea weevils. On California cotton fields, DE was found to be more effective than chemical insecticides and the yield was substantially increased.

No shock setback to field crops after treatment with DE: When chemical insecticides are applied to a plant, there is a shock period for about three to seven days when the plant does little or no growing. Using chemicals several times a year equals many days of no growth. Alternatively, using DE prior to bug infestation keeps plants from spending energy to repair insect damage. Plants can use this energy for lush growth. DE can be systematically applied throughout the growing season.

DE is kinder to bees than chemicals: In many states, chemical pesticide operators are legally required to notify beekeepers 48 hours in advance of aerial spraying to keep from decimating the honey industry. Despite this, it is estimated that over 400,000 (10 percent) of the nations bee colonies are destroyed or damaged annually by chemical pesticides—an unacceptable loss considering that honey bees are responsible for pollinating $3 billion worth of crops each year.

When Diatomaceous Earth is applied to crops or orchards, the honey bee tends to protect themselves by simply avoiding those blossoms already treated with DE. However, if DE does get on a bee's body, it is covered with slick hairs that are able to help prevent dehydration of body fluids. Then the bee simply vibrates its wings rapidly to remove the dust and protect itself. However, should a bee get enough DE on it to cause death, he's the only insect that dies. Even if he makes it back to the hive, he does not contaminate the colony as DE is not a chemical toxin.

How to avoid repelling beneficial insects with DE: Dusts in general are repellent to all insects including beneficial ones, but there is one way to drastically cut back their losses. To ensure more beneficial bugs survive, treat plants with DE at a time when there are fewer of them on the plants, such as early morning, or in the cool of the evening. It is also wiser to apply DE as a fine spray of liquid solution or "slurry" as the beneficial bugs are more sensitive to the airborne powder than the liquid. (See Chapter Five for the liquid solution recipe and method of application).

The benefits of DE as a natural fertilizer: In addition to being an effective natural insecticide, DE doubles as a fertilizer, soil amender, and growth enhancer. When soaked into the soil DE adds 14 beneficial trace minerals. The average DE is approximately 86 to 90 percent silicon dioxide with many other beneficial trace minerals in a readily assimilable form. These trace minerals such as: titanium, boron, manganese copper, calcium, magnesium and zirconium encourage luscious growth. DE also improves percolation and air circulation of the soil, while reducing compaction and water requirements. Some users say their plants grow more luscious especially when an electrostatic sprayer is used. It is thought there is an uptake of nutrients from the DE through the leaves.

Anecdotal User Testimonials:
How DE Protects Crops & Orchards

DE boosts plant growth: Two Californian farmers decided to use the non-polluting insecticide DE for their vast and intensive farming operations with highly favorable results. They explained: "Let's get this straight. I don't believe any of that propaganda about poisons staying on foods and causing sickness and cancers. I've washed the mud off my hands under the spigots of a dozen different poisons. Nothing's wrong with me. But, I love DE better because it increases plant production. Chemicals will poison plants, sealing the leaves so the plant sits there, rather shriveled. By the time it recovers from shock setback, you gotta hit it with another dose of poison. But with DE, it seems the plant starts growing faster after you dust it with DE especially if you use an electrostatic ionizer."

Ionizers make DE stick like glue to plants: A DE enthusiast and user for over 30 years praises and describes the value of using an electrostatic negative-charge ionizer to coat the entire plant with DE, especially making it stick and stay put underneath the leaves. He said, "Some old guys ribbed us about our pride in using our non-toxic DE insecticide. We had a tractor-mounted application unit made for orchards with an electrostatic applicator nozzle that makes any targeted plant, tree, or structure a magnet for DE."

He continues, "One old guy said he had a field we could use to prove to him what we were saying about how good DE was. We had only 20 pounds of DE left and sprayed an area. Three days later I called him to verify. He apologized for the ribbing and verified we not only killed the bugs directly in the area where we sprayed, but it also killed bugs across another 45 degree angle where we didn't even enter the field. He didn't understand why the crop became bug free in that area as well, until I explained there was a stiff breeze that day and the 45 degree angle got covered indirectly with DE due to the wind drift and the magnetic effect of the ionizer."

No toxic residue with DE usage: "As an orchardist I get exceptional results with fruit tree insect control and recommend DE to orchardists anywhere. Since using Diatomaceous Earth I get no toxic chemical residue problems left on the fruit. This makes it possible to do applications if necessary, right up until the day of harvest."

Wormy fruit & tree moths: "DE protects our trees from developing wormy fruit, especially from codling moth, oriental fruit moth, twig borer, aphids and mites, etc. For fruit maggots, trees can be protected by coating the ground around the tree base with a spray of DE and also painting the trunk with an adhesive, then applying DE to it. This treatment reduces migration of Japanese beetle grubs and fruit fly maggots."

Better crop dusting with DE: A crop duster in Arizona who once used chemical insecticides changed his allegiance to DE after skeptically trying out DE for crop insect control. He then declared, "I'll never use a poisonous insecticide again. This non-toxic DE is more effective, causes no plant shock or setback whatsoever, and actually benefits the soil." Although the crops he had protected with DE were not then harvested, he estimated a slightly lower cost for protection than with poisonous products.

Cabbage looper worms don't loaf around in DE: In Texas, a large vegetable broker had DE tested on a bell pepper field that was infested with the cabbage looper worm. The field was divided; one side was treated with parathion, the other with Diatomaceous Earth. The parathion killed almost all the worms in the first few minutes, but the effectiveness dissipated quickly. By the third day, new eggs were being laid in the field, which on the sixth day were hatching on the parathion treated plants, but not on the DE side.

The side of the field treated with Diatomaceous Earth showed complete control after three days. Since DE stays put on the plants, especially when applied with an ionizer, no millers were seen landing or laying eggs. Did the product really work? Time after time, field demonstrations proved the affirmative.

How an orchardist stopped wooly worms with DE: "The only control others farmers have to stop wooly worms is to erect an aluminum edging barrier. To do that on 80-acres costs $400 plus about 12 man-days to install. But all we use is $110 worth of DE and about one man-day of labor. After laying down the DE we saw an army of wooly worms crawling across the dirt road. As they came to the bead of DE dust in the bottom of the trench, most turned back. The few that crawled across and started up the steep bank, lost their hold and fell back into the dust. None went more than 10 feet after getting into the dust before dying in the DE."

Commercial scale success with DE on apple orchard: An organic orchardist from Ontario, Canada, stated: "We have used DE since 1964 in our apple orchards and found it very effective against all harmful insects. In 1982, we grew 10,000 bushels of apples using DE, making it possible for us to get premium prices for our crop. We ship as far away as Pennsylvania."

"Timing is important. We make applications at about 10-day intervals. Of course, by carefully observing insect buildup, application can be made as needed. However, we like to use it in advance of infestation, as it tends to repel the invasion and prevent any damage from taking place."

Comparing the neighbor's trees: A farmer who successfully used DE on his animals, then successfully tried it on his plants and elm trees. He stated: "DE completely stopped the elm beetle on my trees, while the neighbor's untreated trees had a great deal of damage."

DE cheaper and better than chemicals on cotton fields: A crop and cotton field owner stated: "Diatomaceous Earth must be used as a preventive. Plants must be kept covered with DE from the time they break through the ground. We've applied more than $25,000 worth of the DE this summer. To have used poisons would have cost us almost twice as much. The cotton field had to be poison-sprayed every 3 days much of the summer. We have only dusted every 14 days with DE and it has kept the bugs under better control than the poisons."

The First Application: "As an example (in this Colorado area) the first application of DE is made in Winter around the end of February or when there is a short period of warm weather around this time of year. During this warm spell, aphids start to hatch. If not controlled, they will live through the next two months of cold weather and present a much bigger problem in the spring."

The Second Application: "The next application is made in Spring around the middle of April to control the aphids, as well as the first hatch of mites and twig borer which start to infest the orchard. It is very important to get in and make these early applications for aphids and mites so they don't get a chance to build up large populations and do a lot of damage. As soon as a buildup of these insects is noticed an application of DE should be made. Then, careful watch should be maintained in case another buildup starts to occur."

The Third Application: "Excellent control of the twig borer, oriental fruit moth, codling moth, aphids and mites can be obtained in the following manner. About the middle of April we set out traps in the orchard for the codling moth and carefully watch them for buildup to determine when the next application of DE should be made.

The traps are composed of a 1-pound coffee can filled with a mixture of 9-parts water, 1-part molasses and 1 percent sodium benzoate. These are hung from the branches. Five traps are put to every ten acres down the same row. Each night more moths are caught in the traps. We observe when the peak number of coddling moths trapped reaches about 30. Then, the number caught starts to drop each night. Ten to twelve days after the peak is reached, the third application of DE is made. It takes between 8 and 20 days for the eggs laid by the moths to hatch. The moths themselves do no damage, so get after the larvae. By making the DE application 10 days after the peak catch in the traps, you can be sure to have an environment of DE waiting for the moth larvae when they hatch."

The Fourth Application: "This is made about 2 weeks later around the end of May, or beginning of June, on the basis of what is observed in the traps. This application will usually carry through to the end of the season, unless a heavy flight of moths occurs, in which case a **fifth application** will be required. The fourth and fifth applications are directed against the twig borer, the oriental fruit moth and the coddling moths. Again, it is very important to watch the traps. When a peak catch has been made and the catch starts to decline in number, wait ten days and make the application of DE. This plan gives excellent control of these insects."

Red-pine sawfly stands no chance in woods with DE: A graduate student at the University of Maine was trying out an insect infecting bacterium mixed with DE to kill the red-pine sawfly, a caterpillar that was infesting the Maine woods. "We actually weren't expecting to get any results, but when we sprayed DE the first year, we found we had gotten complete control of the red-pine sawfly," recalls Dr. John Dimond, a professor of entomology, who supervised the experiment. "We began to suspect it was the bacteria that was killing the insects, but discovered instead it was Diatomaceous Earth. We went out again the next year with plain Diatomaceous Earth and got the same results! The infestation went away the following year."

Cotton grew one foot higher with DE; only the neighbors had pink bollworm: The Applied Biological Sciences Laboratory, a private lab in Glendale, performed some crop-dusting experiments with cotton. Several fields were sprayed with Diatomaceous Earth, while adjacent fields were treated with chemical pesticides. "With DE, we found we were getting complete control of all insects, including the pink bollworm, which had completely destroyed a field less than a mile away," said Dr. Paul Jewel, a research associate at the lab. Incidentally, the pink bollworm, resists treatment with malathion and must be killed with parathion, an organophosphate so powerful that a single drop in the human eye can be fatal.

"What was most remarkable was the difference to productivity between the fields sprayed with chemical pesticides and those sprayed with Diatomaceous Earth. Both areas had good insect control, but the cotton sprayed with Diatomaceous Earth was growing about a foot higher! The farmers said they expected to get an extra half-bale per acre out of these plants. We were very excited about DE."

Kansas State University successfully tested truck crops: "A number of tests on various vegetable pests revealed very good results with DE, which caused many other organic growers to follow suit."

Whitefly tests—green light to organic growers and DE:
An experiment conducted at the Research and Education Center of the University of Florida found whitefly populations were severely reduced by using DE. They reported that Diatomaceous Earth significantly reduced whitefly adults by 86 to 95 percent on the fifth day after application, which encouraged more organic growers to use DE as a natural insecticide.

An orchardist's success story treating fruit trees with DE:
A commercial orchardist in Colorado successfully uses DE on more than 300 acres of fruit trees: apple, peach, apricot and cherry. To control the bugs he applies the DE with an orchard duster equipped with an electrostatic charging unit to make the dust adhere well, especially to the undersides of leaves.

Most of the dusting was done at night at a cost of about $25 an acre per year. He explained the benefits of spraying fruit trees with DE at night. They include:

- The air is usually calmer at night, so more efficient dusting can be done.

- The polarity of trees at night is such that a better adherence of the electrostatically charged dust particles is achieved.

- Larvae moths do a lot of damage at night. DE dusting at the only time the moth is out prevents propagation.

- The beneficial insect count at night is lower so there will be less damage.

- As an added benefit, this orchardist got a pleasant surprise when he discovered that DE also took control of mildew. Also, by dusting a day or two before harvest, there was no brown rot. Using DE, his insect damage to fruit in one year was only about 2 percent from twig borers and 2 percent from the oriental fruit fly.

While enthusiastic about the effectiveness of DE as an insect repellent, the Colorado orchardist admitted he was pessimistic about the average farmer's willingness to follow such a conscientious program: "Ninety five percent of farmers today don't know about the life cycle of insects. They want someone to tell them when to spray. You've got to get out there and know what's going on. Timing and good knowledge of pests improves DE's success," he said.

Early and conscientious applications at precise timings are the most important factor in achieving results with DE to control a wide variety of destructive orchard insects and wormy fruit without using harmful chemicals. Contact your local County Extension Agent to help you identify insects and get details of their life cycles and when and how to spray. The example of an application schedule provided must be adjusted according to your specific area, season and type of insect problem.

5

Application Tools & Methods For Using Diatomaceous Earth (DE)

Novelty DE Applicators

DE can be used in very small to very large places—a tiny ant entry point into a home, carpeting, pet bed, patio, milk parlor, poultry house, a huge commercial crop of vegetables, or an orchard of fruit trees. Creative imagination goes a long way to get past any resistance of how to apply the powder without commercial applicators. All sorts of things can be used to apply DE such as: a pair of panty hose, a burlap bag, spice jar, pepper shaker, ketchup or mustard bottle with the pop-up nozzle for use in cracks and crevices, flour sieve, colander, mesh strainer, coffee can with holes in the lid, stiff broom, leaf blower, or an aeration fan.

Commercial DE Applicators

A variety of commercial applicators or "dusters" can be utilized for applying DE on pets; in cracks and crevices; on pantry shelves; under heavy appliances; in cupboards, attics, cellars, basements and under foundations; in building construction wall voids; storage sheds; large warehouses; office buildings; food handling establishments;

grain mills; farms, kennels, and trade shows; gardens, lawns, crops and orchards. These tools can be found in hardware and building supply stores, garden nurseries, or from DE distributors, franchises, mail order catalogues or the Internet.

Puffer/squirt bottles: Squeeze type puffer containers or bottles with a crack and crevice nozzle are good applicators for small bug problems especially in the home. One with a thin straw inserted in the top of the can makes it easy to apply DE in hard to reach places. DE can be puffed into the backs of cupboards without having to move items aside, or under heavy appliances such as a stove, refrigerator or dish washer without having to move it.

The Pest Pistol®: Small and simple enough to be used by the home owner, but effective enough to be used by professionals. The Pest Pistol® is a powder applicator effective for treating tiny cracks and crevices to large areas through small openings, and wide coverage in the garden and attic voids. It has an optional extension tube for shooting DE eight feet high.

The tube duster: Best for bigger jobs, especially outside the home. It is long enough to place insecticide on the underside of leaves or reach up to twelve feet high to cover building structures or tree canopies. It will apply dry powder, or spray any liquid. Good ones never clog up.

Hand-crank dust applicators: A very lightweight unit that mounts on the chest with shoulder straps to expel controlled amounts of dust twenty to thirty feet. It is especially effective for gardens and animal barns.

Sandblasting gun: A 1-ton empty bin can be treated in less than a minute. The pressure of the compressed air inlet into the sandblasting gun must be at least 100 psi (pounds per square inch).

Backpack units: Some brands of gasoline-driven backpack units weigh about 22-pounds, having tremendous force, delivering DE about 30-feet. They are excellent when used on a small scale, but would prove unsatisfactory for more than five acres. Growers find them suitable for small groves of fruit trees and big home gardens. Backpacks can apply either dusts or liquids and some are equipped with an electronic nozzle. A backpack electrostatic ionizing unit was demonstrated on the Natural Food and Farming Farm, Atlanta, Texas, on potato bugs. Bugs used to be removed by hand—until the backpack unit put every bug on the ground in 20 minutes.

Aeration fan: For large capacity bins in warehousing facilities, measure out the DE recommended for the size in Chapter Three. Turn on the aeration fan and pour DE into the airflow as fast as the fan will allow. When dust starts blowing out the top of the bin, turn off the fan.

Tractor mounted sprayer units: For treating large acreage on farms, parks, crops or orchards, tractors can be equipped with an electrostatic charged eight-row applicator that makes the DE stick well to the target.

Hose-end sprayer: Buy a hose-end sprayer from a nursery, garden supply or hardware store. Measure 8-ounces of DE and pour into the spray reservoir. Fill to the top with water. Shake the sprayer until no residue is seen on the bottom. Attach the hose and dispense the solution at the rate of 1-2 ounces per 500-square feet, agitating occasionally to prevent residue resettling. DE will begin to work more effectively once dry.

Benefits of DE as a liquid spray: For those who suffer any respiratory condition such as asthma, or for ease of use, the consumer may find it works better to apply DE as a liquid spray or (slurry) rather than sprinkle a dry powder. DE will begin its maximum effect as an insecticide once dry. Be sure to use the unheated amorphous silica, (same as Anti-Caking Agent or Grain Storage Protectant) not the industrial type for swimming pool or fish tank filters.

Recipe for making a DE liquid spray: For every 1-gallon of water, mix 4-tablespoons of DE. Pour the slurry into a standard hand-held trigger spray bottle, or any other liquid spray applicator or spritzer. Obtain one with a large diameter no-clog nozzle, removing any mesh screen. These can be purchased at any garden or hardware store. Pour into smaller spray bottles, or containers from the gallon mix for easier hand-held applications or for storage.

Shake well periodically to ensure even distribution and to prevent DE from settling to the bottom. DE does not dissolve in water, however the particles are suspended in water. Agitation of the container is necessary during application to prevent settling to the bottom of the container and to maintain the strength of the solution.

Target the insecticide onto infested areas. DE will begin working as an insecticide once it is dry. Be careful to avoid spraying liquid into any electrical outlets or motors to avoid electrical shock. Like chemical poisons, DE should be re-applied after rain if it is washed away. Watering should be delayed after an application to give the DE a chance to work. In high humidity DE may be applied more heavily. Some users find liquid DE effective in minutes for uses such as knocking out ants in a mound or on trails. However, fire ants can take a few hours to a couple days to succumb.

Electrostatic spray units: Users of electrostatic spray units vouch they have more bug killing power. These systems can be adapted to hand held hose-end sprayers, knapsacks, tractors and planes. Like iron filings to a magnet, electrostatic equipment vastly improves adhesiveness and coverage of the DE for use in barns, dairies, poultry farms, livestock operations, horse stables, agricultural shows, orchards, crops, greenhouses, nurseries, home gardens, kennels landscape management, golf courses, parks, city sewers, granaries or seed warehouses. Units can be operated from: a tractor battery, a 12-volt lantern battery, a backpack or tractor battery, 12-volt lantern battery, electric or gasoline power, ground rig blower, or crop duster plane.

How Electrostatic Application Systems Work

Anyone who prefers to use the safer non-chemical insecticides but is skeptical about getting good results may certainly think twice and benefit from the following information:

Some types of electrostatic spray systems on ground-operated equipment use a patented air shear component, which produces an electrostatic charge at the nozzle. This charge atomizes liquids into mist-sized droplets. Knapsack units produce a positive charge, whereas the larger ground-operated units produce a negative charge. In either case, the charged spray droplets induce a temporary opposite charge onto the surfaces of certain types of targeted building materials and other grounded (earthed) targets such as: leaves, stems and fruits of growing plants and crops. Because opposite electrical charges attract one another, the target surfaces then pull the large collection of spray droplets to all sides of the chosen objects, including those in dense foliage and those facing away from the direction of the spraying, such as the undersides of leaves.

Factors like humidity and wind speed using conventional application methods affect how well DE sticks to any surface. However, the electrostatic nozzle device solves this problem by forcing the charged particles through the ionized field. Negative electrons from the sprayer will be attracted to a positive surface on the ground and the DE will become firmly attached on all sides without even making a concentrated effort to cover the whole target. Due to the fact that like charges repel, when one area of a surface is covered, it then repels oncoming particles, forcing them to move over and find another place to land.

As soon as the front side of a leaf is covered, the charged dust will move to the back or underside and coat it also. Those who have used the ionizer say this attraction between the plant and the dust is so powerful that a hundred-mile-per-hour wind will not blow away the Diatomaceous Earth.

Further, there is a nutritional advantage to plants resulting in considerable additional growth due to the 14 trace minerals naturally contained in DE. Using an electrostatic device, DE is bonded so tightly to the leaves that it is believed the plant is able to use the minerals by foliar feeding. Dusting without the electronic nozzle does not seem to have the same effect through the leaves, although DE can enrich the soil.

NOTE: Spreading DE on the ground in the spring, then tilling it into the soil will control bugs as they emerge from the pupal stage.

Benefits & Profits Using The
Electrostatic Negative Charge Ionizer

Amongst companies that market DE, there seem to be differing opinions about the effectiveness of using electrostatic negative-charge ionizers to facilitate better coverage, effectiveness and results. Some say it works and some say it's yet to be proven. But those who use it (with proven equipment) will swear by it, especially for getting DE to stick to the undersides of leaves where bugs like to hide.

Below is a collective report and handsome list of benefits generated from users of electrostatic sprayers that will be of interest to those who have larger gardens, orchards, crops, farms, kennels, barns, stables, grain mills, golf courses and health retreats or resorts includes:

- Greatly reduces crop losses where conventional methods fail to reach insects on the undersides of leaves, in dense foliage or under tree canopies. Increases deposits in the upper portion of the tree by 85 percent.

- Vastly increases coverage of the surface area including the undersides of leaves, defying gravity with a wrap-around affect enabling the operator to use lower volumes.

- Increases DE deposits on fruit, avocado, nut orchards, vineyards and other crops by 46 percent.

- Increases the number of mist-sized droplets by 50 percent, in some cases up to ten times more than conventional applicators.

- Increases foliar uptake of mineral nutrients by 31 percent.

- Reduces waste by run-off and air borne drift.

- Reduces the total volume of material applied by airplanes as much as 90 percent and insecticide use by other spray methods by 50 percent. Two or three times as much acreage can be sprayed with a single planeload than when conventional aerial sprayers are used.

- Reduces the conventional aerial rate of 10-gallons per acre to 2-gallons per acre. As few as 5 or 6 nozzles on either side of the boom applicator can reduce the volume to a very low 12-16 ounces per acre representing a big savings to orchardists, crop growers, farmers and other large area or commercial users.

- Reduces the amount of water necessary for mixing insecticides by 50-80 percent, partly due to high velocity air-assistance and atomizing liquids into smaller droplets that are better retained without bouncing away.

- Reduces insecticide costs by an average of 33 percent. Rice farmers can save at least $10 per acre.

- Reduces fuel consumption up to 70 percent.

- Reduces workers exposure to chemicals by 82 percent.

- Significantly increases profits by substantially lowering labor and operating costs through lower volume handling, faster application and time not having to attend to crop failures.

- Reduces the number of planes needed to treat the same acreage, a major savings for aerial applicators.

6

Diatomaceous Earth (DE) Benefits In Products For Humans

Important Caution:

The use of DE for any purpose in this book recommends only food grade DE (pure amorphous "non-crystalline" silicon dioxide) with 0.1 percent ($^1/_{10th}$ of 1 percent) or less "crystalline" silica in accordance with the 1997 recommended OSHA safety standard, and no additives.

Food Grade

Diatomaceous Earth is also known as:

* Anti-Caking Agent

* Animal Feed Additive

* Grain & Seed Storage Protectant

* Trace Mineral Supplement (for humans)

Public Interest For DE In Human Supplements

It's interesting to note that the mineral Diatomaceous Earth is made more readily available for human ingestion in Europe, China, and other countries around the world. DE is used in the health industry as a supplement for various purposes. Although the FDA in USA has not approved DE for human ingestion, people have been using food grade DE in a powder form or capsules for colon cleansing, detoxifying, and as an anti-parasitic. DE is also used to sooth burns and insect bites, and it is used in some cosmetic products such as facemasks and scrubs.

According to an herb store in Austin, Texas, there has been an upsurge of interest and demand, particularly in the last two years for food grade DE for a variety of different health reasons. Consumers are starting to take notice after learning from bird and animal farmers who have been marveling for at least four decades about the many positive health and healing effects that DE has on their animal and bird stock. Hence the author looked into the topic of DE for human use, including ingestion, and what is currently going on in the consumer world. Although this chapter gives both pros and cons, it is by no means a complete summary of DE in the health industry, and it does come with cautions that appear towards the end of this chapter.

Scientific Studies For Use Of DE In Human Health

The predominant and *major* element in Diatomaceous Earth is Silicon Dioxide or silica, which is not a trace mineral. A working definition of *"trace"* is a small quantity significantly less than 1.0 percent of the material in which the substance is contained. The silicon dioxide content of food grade Diatomaceous Earth is mostly around 80-89 percent which means it is a *major mineral*. Other *trace* (or minor) minerals also co-exist with silica such as, calcium, magnesium, iron, potassium, sodium, titanium, boron, manganese, copper and zirconium. These elements should be revealed on the manufacturer's Material Safety Data Sheet (MSDS). Product labels generally refer to these other minor elements in Diatomaceous Earth as *trace mineral oxides.*

Since 1911 French and German doctors and medical scientists reported therapeutic success using silicon dioxide (the major element in Diatomaceous Earth) for treating numerous diseases, some of which include atherosclerosis, arteriosclerosis, hypertension and dermatitis. Now other promising independent research studies have emerged over the past 2 to 3 decades, which are hard to ignore.

In 1972, Dr. Edith Carlisle produced a detailed report on the subject of Diatomaceous Earth's potential nutritional benefits as a source of silicon dioxide. In Chapter 11 of her report, **Biochemistry of the Essential Ultratrace Elements,** on Silicon, she states that this element is essential for bone growth, and nutritionally important for preventing some forms of chronic diseases associated with aging. She noted the aorta, trachea and tendons were 4-5 times richer in silicon than the liver, heart and muscle. Skin and hair also contain unusually large amounts of silicon.

It stands to reason why DE being primarily composed of silicon dioxide is today becoming recognized as having a major role to play in anti-aging, by reversing or preventing the chronic diseases that appear associated with the areas of the body when there is a silicon deficiency.

The only cautionary statement Dr.Carlisle noted in her research was a concern related to the amount of *crystalline* silica contained in Diatomaceous Earth. In 1997, OSHA recommended a threshold of 0.1 percent ($^1/_{10th}$ of 1 percent) as a safety standard in any product containing *crystalline* silica, which is an amount regarded in lab analysis as undetectable.

Adolf Butenandt, the 1993 Nobel Prize winner, proved life is not possible without silica. Humans, animals and plants have an essential need for this mineral to maintain life. Silicon is especially required in our skin, hair, nails, teeth, bones, aorta, lungs, spleen, lymph nodes, blood, bones, cartilage and connective tissue.

In the July/August 1993 journal called: **Nutrition Today**, Louise

Pasteur predicted, "Silicon would be found to be an important therapeutic substance for many diseases."

In 1993, two nutrition research scientists, Carol D. Seaborn, Ph.D., and Forrest H. Nielson, Ph.D., documented in the same journal that silicon is essential for forming and maintaining normal healthy bones, blood vessels, and brains cells, which they believed deserved more attention from the clinical research and medical community. They reported silicon is concentrated more in the growth area of bones, stimulating bone cell and collagen production.

Deficiency of silica resulted in abnormal, immature bone development. Silica was also found to therapeutically reduce the amount of aluminum in brain nerve cells, which is now known to be one of the causes of Alzheimer's disease, senility and dementia, particularly when combined with low dietary calcium, high dietary aluminum, an under-active thyroid, and low estrogen levels.

Two other European scientists Zeller and Odlier, go further to boldly promote "non-crystalline" silicon dioxide as a natural cancer defender. Doctors are now researching the benefits by using silicon dioxide in combination with other cancer therapies because silica has the ability to absorb and eliminate toxic waste products from the body. Silica also strengthens the ability of the connective tissue to form a defense barrier for warding off cancer-causing free radical cells, and helps to prevent degeneration of cells.

The June 1994 issue of **Journal of Nutrition** documented food grade DE (silicon dioxide) as a cholesterol-lowering agent when given in the diet of cholesterol-fed rats. Further studies are needed to determine if inadequate dietary silicon contributes to cardiovascular disease such as ischemic heart disease and hypertension.

Medical science is forever changing—back and forth, then back again, as we have witnessed with multiple drugs, coffee, certain vitamins and the Atkins Diet. Although most doctors are unfamiliar with DE for the purposes mentioned in this book, especially human ingestion, readers should confirm the information in this chapter with other qualified sources. Consumers wishing to use DE internally should also read the product label and package information.

DE Used In Medicine To Treat E.coli

In November, 1994, **Discover** magazine revealed medical scientists had success with Diatomaceous Earth tests against intestinal E. coli, commonly caused by food poisoning. Canadian doctors have been using Diatomaceous Earth (silicon dioxide) especially for children in the early stages of treatment for E.coli food poisoning before it caused irreversible kidney damage.

Dr. Glen Armstrong at the University of Alberta, tested Diatomaceous Earth on healthy volunteers, with no ill effects to stop the E.coli toxin taking hold in the stomach. They found a way to bait the E.coli with a decoy—a sugar molecule lures the toxin in, then binds, and traps the microbe, which sticks very tightly to the DE. The pores in the DE act like a "lobster trap" or a cage, so the E.coli microbe doesn't come out again. The "decoy" process, allows the body about a week to build up antibodies to the bacteria.

Dr Armstrong believes, "There is a window of opportunity in which the decoy will work—during the time the toxin is damaging the intestines, but before the more serious kidney damage occurs." Before the E.coli has a chance to enter a cell in the stomach wall, the toxic bacteria attached to the DE are eliminated from the body because the DE particles are indigestible, although enough trace minerals are absorbed to rebuild the body back to health. For this reason treatment with DE has to be given promptly at the outset and diagnosis of E.coli infection.

Benefits Of DE To Eliminate Intestinal Parasites

Many people have quietly found food grade Diatomaceous Earth is an effective alternative for eliminating parasites from the stomach and intestines where eggs are hatched that may spread throughout the body. Once worms and eggs are eliminated with an intestinal cleansing, many symptoms of general illness and disease often disappear, beginning in just a few days to a week. Before using DE to eliminate internal parasites, it helps to know something about them—including how to avoid re-infestation in the future.

Dr Ross Andersen, a leading USA authority on parasitic infections, who has over 20 years of experience with more than 20,000 patients, believes 85 to 95 percent of people are infected with at least one type of parasite. In an article titled: **Are You Clear Of Parasites?** he warns that we don't usually know we have parasites. Besides, they are mostly overlooked or missed by the medical society. Lab tests only detect about 20 percent (i.e., 40 to 50 types out of the 1,000 species) of parasites which can live in our body but escape laboratory detection. "Doctors are only testing for about 5 percent of the parasites and missing 80 percent of those. This brings the ability to clinically find parasites down to one percent."

As long as parasites remain in the intestines, our immune systems cope with them, but once they escape into other parts of the body, we become highly susceptible to other diseases. Parasites have been known to attach themselves in unsuspecting places such as breast cells, the vulva, uterus and fallopian tubes causing infections. They are capable of destroying calcium in the bones causing arthritic symptoms and eating the myelin sheath off nerve cells, causing physical and mental nervous system breakdown by disruption of the brain-nerve impulse.

Invisible parasites, such as protozoa or amoeba can be extremely dangerous, entering the body through contaminated hands, food and water. Once gaining entry, parasites inhabit the colon, lay eggs, then travel through the blood stream attaching themselves to the cells of organs such as the liver, lungs, and brain. They reproduce in a similar way to bacteria and viruses and can cause infection and swelling of the protective covering of the brain or spinal cord resulting in life threatening conditions such as encephalitis or meningitis.

Geoffrey Lapage, author of **Animals Parasitic in Man** states, "There is no organ, or any part of the human body which is immune from parasite infestation." Large parasites appear as visible worms sometimes up to several inches or 30-50 feet long! They reproduce by laying eggs, usually in the digestive system.

Parasites eat from our body, absorbing food, nutritional supplements, fluid, and in some cases, even our cells, leaving the immune system in a weakened and devitalized state. After becoming infested, parasites can live in the body for as long as thirty years. Some can lay up to one million eggs a day in the intestinal walls, cells or other organs.

As parasites fatten, grow and multiply in our body, they secrete their own toxic wastes into our immune system, which make it to go into acute toxic overload, presenting all kinds of persistent ailments and symptoms, the cause of which is hard to diagnose. Parasites not only rob our bodies of what they need to survive, they steal our health. This toxic overload can be debilitating, such as seen in food poisoning or dysentery.

A chronic parasitic infection that secretes low levels of toxins can eventually create an extremely stressed and weakened immune system over a long period of time. This causes easy susceptibility to various kinds of infections when exposed to other viruses and bacteria from the environment, which are fast becoming immune to all kinds of antibiotics and treatments. Traditional drugs can drive an established parasite into a different organ, such as the brain or heart where they become more resistant and may not be killed or eliminated.

How Do Parasites Enter Our Body?

Parasites such as tapeworms can infest the body through inadequate hand washing or unwashed hands particularly after handling animal fur or feces. Parasite eggs can be transmitted through handling kitty litter, dog fecal matter and animal fur. Dog tape worms can be transferred to humans when they are licked on the hand or face, or through kissing pets especially on the nose or mouth, or sleeping with them. The following example may be a reflection of what is happening to millions of children today. A child who reportedly suffered from wheezing, coughing, depression, and allergies to many foods, mold, and dust, found the symptoms diminished after he and the two dogs that he lived with were all diagnosed and treated for parasites.

You can also get parasites from a variety of contaminated foods and water. Parasites are easily and frequently acquired by eating undercooked meat or fish. Parasites can also come from unwashed and undercooked or raw vegetables such as spinach, lettuce and sprouts, and any raw fruit including melons. Parasites on fruits and vegetables can be spread by contaminated water; infested soil; manure fertilizers (which of course are animal feces); sewerage contamination; the dirty unwashed hands of workers; poor unhygienic sanitation in harvesting, packaging and storage, coupled with hot weather, inadequate cooling facilities and lengthy transportation. All these reasons can encourage the increase of parasite population by multiplying in the same way viruses do, or from eggs hatching.

You can also be contaminated with parasites that cause food poisoning by wiping counter tops with unclean dish sponges which harbor bacteria (as Tui Rose mentions in another of her books, **Green, Thrifty & Safer Everyday Home Solutions.**

Parasite eggs can also be inhaled from dry dust and air, or ingested by hugging, shaking hands, sharing a drinking vessel, kissing (even on the cheek), and intimate sexual contact. Parasites can enter cracks or cuts in the skin, especially the feet where the soil and water is contaminated.

Couples can infect each other. When one is diagnosed and treated, their partner should also be treated at the same time. Their children also may be infected from parental contact and will require treating. If there are pets, they should also be treated along with the children and adults. Wherever pets sleep and play, also treat the bedding, romping area, and their fur with food grade DE.

How Does DE Work As An Antiparasitic?

Although human consumption regimes are not accepted (in USA) by the Food and Drug Administration (FDA), they approve the same food grade DE for use in grains for human consumption. We have probably all been eating DE in our food for decades. DE is added in some milling and storage processes to protect grains, legumes, nuts and seeds against moisture and insects such as weevils. It is a matter of choice by the granary or seed mill whether they use food grade DE, toxic chemicals, or some other method of treating our food.

When ingested, pure 100 percent DE has a scrubbing, absorbing and flushing action in the whole digestive system including the large and small intestine. The microscopic particles of porous ground silica particles have the capacity to abrade, absorb and dehydrate the eggs and worms, pulling those through that have set up house inside the host. Therefore, when taking DE, worms may not always be seen in the elimination. However, there should be some noticeable improvement felt by the second day when diarrhea may slow down and abdominal pains subside somewhat, but it could take up to 90 days of flushing with DE to be significant.

Detoxifying And Cleansing The Colon With DE

Dr, Galen Ph.D., author of **Immune System Care and Feeding** suggests for detoxifying and cleansing the intestine with Diatomaceous Earth, increase "from about a teaspoon to a rounded tablespoon over a few days or weeks." Increase slowly to help avoid a detoxifying "healing crisis." Mixing the DE in water "before bed or first thing in the morning if one doesn't normally eat an early breakfast, will allow the DE time to move through and absorb toxins from the digestive tract without interference, and without absorbing medicines or nutrients from foods or liquids." DE can be mixed in water, juice, milk, oatmeal or a smoothie and the taste is barely discernable.

It has been suggested that DE should be used 10 days on and 10 days off for up to 90 days. DE is taken on an empty stomach one hour before taking medication or eating food, or 2 hours after meals morning and night. It is important NOT to miss a single dose to prevent the possibility of re-infection if all parasites and larvae have not been removed.

The highly absorptive properties of this powder helps flush out heavy metals and other chemical toxins within the body with the help of *plenty of water,* which also helps prevent constipation from the drying effect of DE, and to encourage regular and complete elimination.

Remember, parasites are very tenacious and hardy—in order to get rid of them, one has to be very consistent and persistent to continue eliminating new larvae which may hatch into more parasites.

If your doctor is unfamiliar with using Diatomaceous Earth as an anti-parasitic give him/her a copy of this book and ask for guidance or to oversee your care if you intend to follow any regime in this chapter.

David Pitman, author of an article titled: **A Back To The Future Product,** uses food grade DE himself and found that using boiling distilled water helps dissolve the Diatomaceous Earth better. He believes this method could possibly aid in more absorption of the silicon dioxide (silica), and the 14 trace minerals from the stomach into the bloodstream.

Precautions For Ingesting DE

Since DE is highly absorptive, it is best to take it on an empty stomach with plenty of water, then wait an hour or two before eating or taking any medication. Although the majority of ingested silica passes harmlessly and unchanged through the digestive tract, a small part of the trace mineral silicon dioxide is dissolved and absorbed in the stomach wall, then it passes into the blood circulation where it is eventually eliminated in the urine by the kidneys.

Under normal health conditions, kidneys eliminate much larger doses of silicic acid than what they take in. Nevertheless, everything including water can be harmful if not taken in moderation. Avoid prolonged ingestion of excessively high intakes of Diatomaceous Earth, particularly if the *antacid milk of magnesia (magnesium trisilicate—which also contains silica), is* concurrently ingested over a prolonged period of time for digestive problems, or if *the kidneys are not functioning normally.*

The consumer must inquire directly with the manufacturer and distributor regarding the specific composition of their products as Diatomaceous Earth products can vary greatly in quality and suitability for uses. Since clinical experience and research is always evolving and broadening, check the author's website for any further help that may arise, and for any new *anecdotal* comments by users of DE.

Other Interesting Facts About DE For Humans

What is so amazing about DE is that this pre-historic late bloomer can kill insects, while simultaneously enhancing our health when ingested, appropriately and *not excessively* as a natural nutritional supplement. Who could say that about synthetic chemical insecticide poisons, which are generally very harmful or deadly to the body, when ingested, inhaled or absorbed through the skin?

The question arises, if Diatomaceous Earth is classified as a biologically *inert* (not active) substance, how is it absorbed by the body? The insoluble part of Diatomaceous Earth cannot dissolve, and acts like a sweeper in the intestine. As the DE moves throughout the digestive tract, it attracts, binds, and carries away chemical and microbial toxins in the elimination process of the stool.

The anecdotal user comments sprinkled throughout other chapters of this book, come from ranch, kennel, poultry and animal owners, who vouch for the healthy effect upon the animal's skin, joints, hair, eyes, milk production, vitality, and general health, proving even if DE is biologically inert, the body has a way of absorbing a small percentage of the trace minerals to cause a noticeably healthy anti-aging effect when fed in the diet.

Slowly, people are catching on to the benefits of DE for themselves after having observed the amazing animal health phenomenon for at least half a century. In this way, hundreds of thousands of animal owners and veterinarians all across the USA who have been using DE for decades, have been our unofficial but practical researchers. Only recently, has our health and nutrition industry been taking note of the results seen in the agricultural industry.

Diatomaceous Earth exists naturally in abundance in the USA where it is extracted in open-pit mines. Still it remains virtually untapped for human health. Only a few scientists have researched the benefits of ingestion of DE as a natural trace mineral for human health and anti-aging.

What is preventing Diatomaceous Earth from really taking off in the health industry is partially the enormous cost of research. At least one American manufacturer of DE estimates that it would cost $10 million and take ten years to complete research, which in the end "might" allow them to make health benefit "claims" on labels and in advertising.

The delay is said by others to be in no small part due to the force of the chemical and pharmaceutical industries keeping a predominance of toxic chemicals on retail shelves. Additionally, an abundance of government red tape, specifically the Environmental Protection Agency (EPA), and Food and Drug Administration (FDA) have such stringent and costly registration and labeling requirements for DE that DE manufacturers and distributors find it discouraging.

Some of the other obstacles that prevent DE from really taking off are related to the confusion in labeling terminology. These issues are further described in *Chapter Eight* to help you understand the different kinds of DE, and to help select the highest and most appropriate quality of DE for health.

The author cautions, that since a safe level of DE for human consumption has not been "officially" established, long-term ingestion without further research or medical supervision is not advisable. Any one of the 13 or 14 elements in DE may cause an imbalance in the body on a long-term uninterrupted basis, although it does not appear to have been detrimental in almost 50 years with regular farm animal feeding.

The U.S. Food and Drug Administration (FDA) has not approved any of the author's comments for human use. Alternatively, the FDA does not prohibit DE manufacturers from producing and selling DE nutritional mineral supplements for human health as long as the label and website do not make any "claims." There is a catch-22 situation in having an FDA approval for any substance. For decades medical professionals have been misled innumerable times into believing an approved researched substance is safe enough, despite proven and published "potential" side effects. For example, a popular bone building drug Fosamax is now known to cause serious side effects such as bone necrosis and a poorer quality of increased bone density which does not heal well when fractured. We often hear of FDA approved substances being removed from the market after they have been found to be unsafe and already caused harm or death.

The author finds it inadequate and very frustrating that currently you cannot read the (crystalline) silica content on any DE labels. Believe it or not, this vital information has been prohibited from being revealed on all product labels by the Environmental Protection Agency and the State Department of Agriculture who both register Diatomaceous Earth products for grain and animal use. *(See Chapter Eight for more information on how to find out about the crystalline silica content in DE).*

If you are not sure about ingesting Diatomaceous Earth—until there is more research or FDA approval, (which could take a minimum of one decade), there are hundreds of other natural and safe tips in *Chapters Two, Three and Four* of this book for using food grade DE in a multitude of external and non-toxic ways—in the home and garden, on pets, in grains, on farms, crops and orchards, and around buildings.

DE's Role In The Cosmetic & Beauty Industry

DE (silicon dioxide) is now used in the cosmetic industry as an ingredient in a cream base to reflect light away from wrinkles. Although the visual anti-aging effects last only until the face is washed, Hollywood stars are using it as an alternative to surgery or botox injections. Using nanotechnology Diatomaceous Earth is fractionated into billions of microscopic nano-prisms. These extremely small crystal molecules bend, break up or deflect white light into colored light, which has the ability to distort, deceive and alter what the eye sees. After using the cream, the premise is a wrinkle that was once visible becomes less visible.

DE In Facial Cleansing Masks

DE is popular especially in the United Kingdom and Europe in mixed facial mask formulations for the treatment of acne and oily skin. Diatomaceous Earth rich in natural sea algae minerals is absorbed by the skin and is said by beauty chemists to sooth redness, irritation and itchiness (if dryness is not the cause). DE helps draw out acne impurities by osmosis, and absorbs and dries up excess oil. Since DE can be too drying for some, moisturizing should follow cleansing masks.

DE In Exfoliating Facial Scrubs

Diatomaceous Earth is used in detoxifying facial scrubs which are massaged in and left on for several minutes, once or twice a week. The scrub cleanses while it absorbs impurities and exfoliates dead skin cells that dull the skin, bringing freshness to the complexion.

7

Health Risks Linked To
Toxic Pesticides

**Medical, Scientific & Journal Reports
Of Illness & Disease
Caused by Chemical Toxins**

&

Why Diatomaceaous Earth Is Safer

The World Health Organization (WHO)

In a press release on Sept 24, 2004, the WHO announced that chemical pesticides are designed to destroy living organisms, therefore creating hazards for human and animal health, and the environment. Of the 70,000 chemical substances on the market since 1940, a significant number are synthetic pesticides. Worldwide pesticide production doubled between 1970 and 1985. Sales rose from an annual US $2,700 million in 1970, to US $40,000 million. at the end of the century.

Children are facing high risks from pesticide poisoning. Better protection from exposure to toxic contaminants and increasing awareness is needed, and it is especially crucial for both the pregnant and breast feeding mother. When a pregnant mother is exposed to pesticides, the fetus also becomes exposed in the womb. Babies and small children can also come into contact with poisons through breast feeding.

Children are more vulnerable as they explore their environment, playing close to the ground and putting things in their mouth, receiving significant doses of pesticides from soils, dusts and contaminated objects that can be found in their homes or gardens. Also, newborn babies with their weaker immune systems and lungs not fully developed, and small children breath faster than adults, which puts them at higher risk of inhaling more airborne pesticides than adults.

Acute pesticide poisoning has clinical manifestations similar to many common diseases with signs and symptoms not easily diagnosable during the physical exam. Due to this lack of proper diagnosis and treament, pesticide poisoning as the cause of death is often not recognized.

Knowledge of the person's exposure to occupational or environmental factors is of vital importance for diagnosis, treatment, and rehabilitation, as well as for public health purposes. It is essential to obtain an adequate history of any occupational or environmental exposure that may cause or exacerbate a health problem so that a search is permitted for other cases in the family, workplace, or community and to obtain environmental data. Website: www.searo.who.int/en/Section23/Section1326_7472.html

National Poison Prevention Week Council

In 2002, U.S. poison-control centers reported approximately 2.3 million poisonings. Approximately 90 percent of these poisonings occurring in the home involved common household chemical items and pesticides. In a promotion, the U.S. Consumer Product Safety Commission has issued a poison lookout checklist, which highlights areas of the home that are common sites of unintentional poisonings and how to correct situations that might lead to poisonings. The national toll-free phone number for Poison Control Centers is: 1-800-222-1222.

See the checklist at: http://www.cpsc.gov/cpscpub/pubs/383.html

It is not enough to believe a statement on a toxic chemical pesticide label that commonly says: "Safe if used in accordance with label instructions." This is dangerous to assume. People should be cautioned—even if gloves, masks, and protective clothing are carefully used for application, and the spray container is safely put away, still more health damage can occur to other occupants long afterwards. Poisonous chemical pollutants may linger for years on surfaces, clothing, carpets, furnishings, toys, pets, food and also in the air and water, as revealed in many reports published by some of America's top medical and environmental scientists, physicians, health foundations, educational institutes, prestigious news and research journals, as well as many government agencies.

Chemical pesticides act in a multitude of ways including as endocrine disruptors or nerve toxins. They can chronically or permanently be damaging to the blood and tissues, and the nervous, immune endocrine (hormonal), and reproductive systems, as well as organs, such as the brain, heart, lungs, liver, kidneys, pancreas and skin. Chemical pesticides are taken into the body by any of three ways: *breathing, ingestion,* or *absorption* though the skin. Toxicity occurs either in an acute exposure or accumulation from chronic exposures, even in low doses over weeks, months or years and is frequently difficult to diagnose as it can mimic other diseases.

Symptoms Of Exposure To Toxic Pesticides

Acute Exposure: blurred vision, dizziness, confusion, breathing difficulties, heart irregularities, twitching, seizures, numbness, exhaustion, "foggy brain," headache, unsteady gait, nausea, vomiting, diarrhea, skin rash, swelling including in the throat, and unconsciousness. NOTE: This is only a partial list.

Chronic Exposure: sexual and reproductive disorders in both men and women, miscarriage, fetal abnormalities, premature birth, stillbirth, mood and behavioral changes, endocrine disorders, asthma, allergies and other respiratory diseases, nose bleeds, migraines, skin diseases, chronic fatigue, loss of weight and appetite, memory loss, neuropathy (such as numbness, tingling, weakness, painful burning in limbs, hands or feet), and encephalopathy (degeneration of the brain).

Chronically, the blood and organs can become diseased resulting in pernicious anemia, leukemia, lymphoma and other cancers including brain tumors, degenerative diseases including auto-immune diseases, onset of diabetes, Parkinson's disease, Alzheimer's disease, Attention Deficit Hyperactive Disorder (ADHD), and epilepsy to name just a few. NOTE: this is only a partial list.

Of greatest concern is pesticide poisoning to the unborn child, babies, growing children of all ages, and of course pregnant mothers. Chemical toxins can find their way into our genetics and be passed on to future generations resulting in permanent alteration, (including before conception and during pregnancy). Any one, or all of the following seven **detrimental "D's"** can occur): **DNA damage;** (birth) **defects;** (childhood growth) **deformities;** (learning and growth) **developmental delays;** (physical or mental) **disabilities, diseases** and **death.** Sadly, most of these medical conditions and the rather alarming following facts could be eliminated if Diatomaceous Earth was used routinely in a widespread fashion as opposed to chemical toxins on both a short and long term basis.

Alan Giuliano, Ph.D. March 2001, reports symptoms of pesticide poisoning developed by school children. Schools across the country use millions of pounds of toxic pesticides in their locker rooms, kitchens, cafeterias, classrooms and play areas. Children in primary grades all the way through secondary schools and in colleges have been reported to suffer symptoms that include: headaches, dizziness, muscle cramps, learning disabilities, trouble concentrating, irritability, nausea, vomiting, sore throats and eyes, ear problems, skin rashes, blisters, nose bleeds, regression to bed wetting, tiredness and fatigue, breathing problems, asthma attacks, low grade fevers, and depression.

Pesticide Action Network:
Head Lice Treatment Toxic To School Governor

A year after a 64 year old British school principal used an insecticide treatment for head lice she continued to suffer with a numb torso and arms after using a medically recommended head lice product and followed the packet instructions. She urged parents to use non-chemical methods of head lice control on children.

Dr. Sarah Myhill, a UK family practitioner who specializes in organophosphate sheep-dip poisoning, said the symptoms were typical of peripheral neuropathy. This disorder of the nervous system affects the sensory and motor nerves known to occur in acute chemical poisoning, which can be caused by a single lice treatment.

Newsweek:
What's Killing The Frogs?

Fred Guterl reported on May 13, 2002, that scientists are learning frogs can be used to help warn us about dangerous chemical pesticides just as coal miners used canaries to warn them of lethal gases. An ecologist for the U.S. Geological Survey found most of the frogs he chased as a boy had gone and tadpoles were born with deformities including anywhere from 1 to 10 legs. He concluded the cause was pesticides that drifted and then became deposited into the sediment of lakes and ponds.

The findings worried scientists about the implications on animal and human health when chemicals were ingested, inhaled, or absorbed through the skin, affecting the nervous and endocrine systems and other vital bodily functions, even at low doses of exposure.

Another study by a biologist at the University of California, Berkeley, reported in proceedings of the National Academy of Sciences that trace amounts of a common herbicide called atrazine can act as an endocrine disrupter causing disruption to normal secretion of natural hormones. The study found that when tadpoles were exposed to atrazine they developed deformed legs and genitals.

The Lymphoma Foundation Of America (LFA): *Do Pesticides Cause Lymphoma?*

A May 2001, comprehensive review of a worldwide research study, revealed mounting evidence that pesticides are a cause of lymphoma. The report was thoroughly reviewed by nationally recognized scientists, doctors, and health professionals. Reviews of the evidence collected from 117 scientific studies make the correlation between lymphoma and pesticides hard to ignore. The report also included a layman's section with ways to avoid pesticide exposures.

The Lymphoma Foundation of America states that *Lymphoma is the second fastest rising cancer in the United States,* and is now recognized by the LFA as an epidemic. Lymphoma is a cancer of the immune system. It strikes both adults and children, with men being at the highest risk. One study indicates when pesticides are used inside homes lymphoma rates in children are higher. The Lymphoma Foundation of America, is a non-profit national organization devoted to helping lymphoma patients and their families. Visit their website at: *www.lymphomaresearch.org*

To obtain a copy of *Do Pesticides Cause Lymphoma?* write to: Lymphoma Foundation of America, P.O. Box 15335, Chevy Chase, MD 20825. To contact a LFA spokesperson, or to reach doctors who treat lymphoma, call 202-518-8047 or 703-525-2076. Visit their website at: http://psrmabo@igc.org

Doctors' Training On Chemical Toxins In Children

In April 2001, highly qualified doctors gathered for a training session after scientific evidence showed that exposure to common household and environmental chemicals can contribute to the development of neurological and childhood development disorders, such as: Attention Deficit Disorder (ADD), autism, learning disabilities, and brain defects. The workshop revealed the following disturbing facts and focused on medical interventions to reduce neuro-toxic threats throughout life.

- 90 percent of children carry detectable urinary residues of a pesticide that can harm brain development!

- Pesticide flea treatments on pets can expose a young child to *500 times the safe exposure limit for a neuro-toxic pesticide!*

- Over 99 percent of commercial chemicals have <u>not</u> been *tested* in accordance to EPA standards for their effects on brain development.

The joint medical training session hosted in New York included the following groups: The New York Medical Academy, The Center for Childrens' Health, The Environment of the Mt. Sinai School of Medicine, Physicians for Social Responsibility, The Greater Boston Physicians for Social Responsibility, and The JSI Center for Environmental Health Studies.

Grand Rapids Press:
Study On Toxicity In Humans

On March 22, 2001, this article revealed that babies have detectable levels of poisons in their blood streams from birth. By adulthood we have accumulated a scientific estimate of at least 500 chemicals in our bodies!

Optimal Wellness Center:
Pesticides Linked To Miscarriage

Dr Joseph Mercola reveals that mothers who live within 1-square mile of areas sprayed with poisonous pesticides have more miscarriages. The fetus is particularly vulnerable to birth defects in the first two months of pregnancy when the organs are forming. http://www.mercola.com/2001/feb/28/pesticides_miscarriage.html

Carpets Harbor Toxic Dust

A May 2001, interview in the *New Scientist* with an environmental engineer John Roberts revealed that a typical sample of household carpet dust contained high levels of chemical contaminants including pesticides. Chemical toxins are tracked inside the home on footwear. They become trapped in carpet fibers—the largest reservoir of dust in the house. The engineer suggested vacuuming the carpets up to 25 times a week for a few weeks to reduce deep dust levels and allow vacuuming to be scaled back to as little as four times a week. In one home, lead levels in the carpet were reduced from over 18 times the official safety threshold to 13 times below in 14 months. He also suggested buying a high-quality doormat, or better still, leave all shoes at the door. Further, a house with bare floors and a few area rugs will have about one-tenth of the dust found in a house with wall-to-wall carpet.

In another report, the *New Scientist* published that an EPA study revealed that household pesticide levels increased *400 times* by contamination when trodden in on the feet of people and pets. This is because carpets are protected from exposure to sunlight and rain that would normally help to break down pollutants.

Discovery Health Channel:
"Toxic Legacies"

We all acquire traces of industrial chemicals and pesticides regardless of how careful we are about what we eat and drink. Chemical toxins known as endocrine disruptors become trapped in our fatty tissues, causing our own hormone signals to be disrupted. If hormone levels are disrupted during embryonic development, the bones and muscles may not develop properly. Further, the full impact may not materialize in boys and girls until puberty when their sexual organs finish developing. Website: http://health.discovery.com/premiers/toxic/inside.html

Environmental Science & Technology:
Study Finds Toxic Soup In Household Air & Dust

A comprehensive study published September 2003, was conducted by a team of environmental toxicology scientists for the **Silent Spring Institute.** The study of toxins in homes found alarming levels of some of the most commonly used chemicals and pesticides containing endocrine-disruptor compounds including some that had been banned for more than ten years!

On average, in the homes studied, dust contained 26 different chemicals. There were 19 chemicals found in air samples. Most homes had at least one chemical that exceeded the EPA's exposure guidelines, which may explain the **Center for Disease Control's** (CDC's) findings that children aged 6-11 have higher pesticides exposure levels than the rest of the population.

A 1990 peer-reviewed EPA study found that indoor concentrations were generally higher than outdoors. People spend a large portion of their time indoors where sources of chemicals, coupled with limited ventilation, no wind, rain or sun, and slow chemical degradation processes cause increased pollutant concentrations.

Toxicity effects related to the endocrine system are limited and not considered in EPA guidelines. Chemicals and pesticides containing endocrine disruptor compounds found in homes are highly toxic and pose significant health risks. They are believed to block, mimic or disrupt the normal function of hormones that are essential for the healthy development and function of cells and tissues. They have been linked to neurological, developmental and reproductive health problems. In addition there is insufficient scientific and analytical data to determine the risks of exposure to "combinations" of toxic chemicals found in nearly every household sampled. Visit the silent spring institute website at: *www.silentspring.orghttp://pubs3.acs.org/acs/journals/doilookup? in_doi=10.1021/es0264596*

American Cancer Society

UniSci Daily University Science, cited research that was published in the international journal *CANCER*, (December 1, 2000): In a study of children exposed to household insecticides and professional extermination methods within the home, it was found that they are *three to seven times* more likely to develop Non-Hodgkins Lymphoma (NHL) compared with children who have not been exposed to pesticides. Additionally, household insecticides increased the risk of Lymphoblastic Lymphoma by *12.5 times*. The study found that a child's risk of developing NHL was similar for both maternal exposures to pesticides during pregnancy (in utero) and direct (postnatal) exposure to pesticides including weed & rodent killers, and fungicides. Website: http://unisci.com/

Pesticide Action Network:
Pesticides In People

A report on February 14, 2003, revealed that studies released in January 2003 by the Center For Disease Control (CDC) indicated that 19 of the 34 pesticides tested were detected in the blood or urine of test subjects. Research shows that surprisingly low levels of exposure to chemical pesticides in the developing fetus in the womb or young children can cause irreversible damage if the exposure occurs when certain organs or systems are in a critical stage of development. The effects of this damage such as infertility or damage to the reproductive system may not become apparent until later in life. To view the CDC's second national report on human exposure to environmental chemicals, visit:
http://www.cdc.gov/exposurereport/

Scottish Scientists Link Pesticides To Childhood Leukemia

A study by a team of Scottish scientists linked childhood leukemia to pesticides widely used in many countries. The study looked at the exposure histories of 136 mothers from around the world who gave birth to children who developed acute infant leukemia and compared them with 266 mothers who had healthy babies. They found that pregnant women, who were exposed to certain pesticides, were *ten times* more likely to have a baby with leukemia than mothers who were not exposed! Visit Website: http://scotlandonsunday.com/news.cfm?id=SS01013063&feed=N

Panups:
Organic Food Proves Less Chemicals in Kids

August 2, 2002: Evidence shows that children who eat more organic food have fewer chemicals in their bodies. Visit website: http://www.panna.org/resources/panups/panup_20020802.dv.html

National Post:
Poisoning Our Grandchildren

An article by Veronique Mandal, April 24, 2004, revealed that according to researcher Dr. Margaret Sanborn, of The Ontario College of Family Physicians, "the devastating effects of pesticide poisons are making their way into the genetics of our grandchildren. It is becoming very clear that the effects of even extremely low levels of pesticides on humans are very, very serious."

New research indicates that home use of pesticides is linked to a myriad of cancers. Pesticide exposure was found to have a strong association with increased rates of leukemia and cancer, particularly of the brain, prostrate, pancreas and lymph. Women in various agriculture sectors have increased incidences of breast cancer and people employed in agriculture from farmers to chemical producers, have the greatest exposure risks to disease. Higher rates of Parkinson's and Lou Gehrig's disease are believed to be caused by exposure to pesticides.

The children of pregnant mothers exposed to home and garden insecticides (including flea and tick products), and occupational insecticides and herbicides had a significantly increased risk of birth defects, brain and kidney tumors, acute leukemia and Non-Hodgkin's lymphoma.

The Hamilton Spectator:
Doctors Warn Chemicals Equal Disease

On April 24, 2004, Suzanne Morrison reported that Ontario family doctors urged limiting the use of common pesticides. A major study strongly linked pesticides to deadly diseases and ailments such as: severe effects on the nervous system, higher rates of depression, suicide, learning disabilities, birth defects, poor fetal growth, fetal death, infertility, cancers of the prostate, kidney and pancreas, Non-Hodgkins lymphoma and leukemia. Children and the unborn fetus are subject to greater risk if they are exposed through their parents' association with agricultural, occupational, indoor and outdoor lawn and garden pesticides. Contaminated or exposed work clothing should be kept and washed separately from family clothing.

Of course the pesticide industry objected to the conclusions, but did agree on the need to improve understanding of safe handling practices and the risks to children from exposure to domestic pesticides. Dr. Margaret Sanborn, one of the researchers, responded that the pesticide industry might be concerned about experiencing a financial impact from the review's findings. However, she hoped they would research healthier alternatives. "Doctors are more worried about their patients' health than about financial impacts on the chemical industry," Dr. Sanborn concluded.

Dr. S. Epstein—Cancer Prevention Coalition: *Cancer: A Growth Industry*

The incidence of cancer has escalated to epidemic proportions over recent decades, now striking nearly *one in every two men, and over one in every three women* in their lifetimes. David Ross reported that Dr. Samuel Epstein, professor emeritus of environmental medicine at the University of Illinois School of Public Health, and Chairman of the Cancer Prevention Coalition (CPC), predicted by the year 2050 the growth rate of cancer will have doubled.

Dr. Epstein blamed the rise in cancer on carcinogenic chemicals in three categories of consumer products: 1) food, 2) cosmetics and toiletries, 3) household goods. He was particularly concerned about the very risky use of home and garden pesticides. Major excesses of childhood cancers are found where pesticides are used in the home, yard or garden. Even pet collars pose risks—those that contain chemicals are highly likely to be contaminated with carcinogens. Exposed dogs have a five times greater risk of getting canine lymphoma.

Occupational exposures to pesticides are a major cause of cancer in men and to a lesser extent, breast cancer in women. Children whose parents work with pesticides, and who carry those toxins into their home exposing mothers during pregnancy, have major excesses of childhood cancers after these carcinogens are absorbed into their bloodstream. However, with education these carcinogens can be avoided to help reduce the risk of cancer. For more information visit the website: http://www.preventcancer.com/publications/pdf/ Interview percent 20 percent 20Jun percent 2003.html

Multiple Chemical Sensitivities (MCS):
A Link To Cancer In Kids

Dr. Marion Moses' book, **Designer Poisons,** declares there is no young person alive today who has not been born without some exposure in the womb to synthetic chemicals, which can disrupt development. She says strong evidence suggests that chemicals can affect the health and sexual functioning of offspring if "either" parent had been exposed to toxic chemicals.

Toxins reach the womb not only through contaminants that the mother takes during pregnancy, but also those that accumulated in her body throughout her life *before* pregnancy. The Sierra Club states there are approximately 200 chemicals in the average person's body fat.

The developing neurological systems of children make them especially vulnerable to permanent damage from the effects of chemicals. One study suggested that lawn sprays could cause a four-fold increase of cancer in children.

Many chemically related diseases are difficult to diagnose. The National Academy of Sciences reveal at least 15 percent of the population has MCS, sometimes called *environmental illness* (EI) or *chemical allergy*. MCS is a chronic health condition.

Dr. Sherry Rogers, M.D., author of **Tired or Toxic** is also a sufferer of MCS. She taught advanced courses in environmental medicine and likens MCS sufferers to the canaries used in mines to detect dangerous gases. MCS sufferers warn that certain substances are toxic for everyone. Nobody is immune and anyone can develop chemical sensitivity, even after only one chemical exposure, or if the detoxification pathways are weakened from previous exposures. Symptoms may not appear for days, weeks, months, or even many long years after exposure.

Globe And Mail:
Unlabelled Substances In Pesticides

An article by Martin Mittelstaedt, June 9, 2001, reported: Pesticide manufacturers are required only to identify the "active" ingredients on their product labels—often with little or no disclosure required for "inert" ingredients. In a federal government list of roughly 5,000 "inert" ingredients, most of them, (even some suspected carcinogens), are not listed on pesticide labels as "inert" ingredients because they are considered "trade secrets." Consumers are left surprisingly in the dark about inert ingredients which may comprise anywhere from 1 to 99 percent of a pesticide product. http://www.theglobeandmail.com/

The author cautions consumers: Inert ingredients are frequently used as fillers. According to the WHO, unnamed *inert ingredients* can be even more toxic than the prime named ingredient. *Inert ingredients* contain a wide variety of substances. Although there are many unusual but seemingly harmless ingredients found in pesticides such as breadcrumbs, bran, apple jelly, gum, fragrances, perfumes and dyes, on the other hand other inert ingredients are laced with toxic compounds that can cause cancer, birth defects and other harmful effects as seen below.

The New York Attorney General:
Secret Hazards Of Inert Ingredients In Pesticides

In February 1996, the Attorney General released eye opening public information on toxic chemical pesticides including *inert ingredients*. Most people have a misconception that *inert* substances are safe, inactive, neutral, non-toxic non-reactive, powerless, or are harmless to health or the environment. This is far from the truth. *Inert ingredients* can be dangerous chemicals, linked to long-term health problems like nervous system disorders, liver and kidney damage, birth defects, and much more.

The EPA often reclassifies inert ingredients after they have been on the market for some time. For example, according to the EPA Federal Register entitled: *Reclassification of Certain Inert Ingredients* (March 8, 2002), a meeting was held on reclassification recommendations for upgrading the toxicity status of certain inert ingredients from "Potentially Toxic Inerts/High Priority for Testing" to List 1 "Inerts of Toxicological Concern." The EPA also intended to downgrade the toxcity status and reclassify the inert ingredient, Rhodamine B, from List 1 to List 4B, which states *"Inerts for which the EPA has sufficient information to reasonably conclude that the current pattern of use in pesticide products will not adversely affect public health or the environment."*

Currently there is no government rule that forces manufacturers to list each and every *inert ingredient* as they are regarded as "Trade Secrets." The NY Attorney General states, "This information is simply too important to keep secret any longer because what the public does not know now about pesticides may very well hurt them some day."

Modern technological laboratory analysis claims many of the *inerts* are indeed toxins. Some are even categorized as "hazardous substances," such as chloroethane, a suspected carcinogen. Other so-called inert ingredients are: chloroform, cresol, benzene, dibutylphthalate, dimethylphthalte, hexane, methyl bromide, rhodamine B, and toluene to name just a few. It's very concerning that insecticide products registered by the EPA are allowed to contain one or many of the hundreds of toxic chemicals under the protection of trade secrets—they do not need to be listed individually by law on the insecticide product label. The consumer (whom could be pregnant or may have a baby and young children at home) is left totally in the dark when deciphering confusing, deceptive, vague and generalized labeling terms such as *inert ingredients*. This is most unfortunate and dangerous—as consumers have no idea what poisons they are buying that will lurk as destructive forces in and around their homes, exposing family members and pets. Further, these toxic chemical insecticide products do not come with package inserts or hazards disclosure fact sheets like those given out with pharmaceutical drugs, which inform consumers of the ingredients, potential dangers, and known side-effects. This needs to be changed.

The chemicals used as *inert ingredients* include some of the most dangerous substances known. Although different inert ingredients have different side-effects, they are known to cause a combination of any one of the following wide range of detrimental health conditions such as: nausea, dizziness, fatigue, skin and eye irritation, burns, inflammation, abdominal pain, muscle atrophy, anorexia, convulsions, fetal resorption, respiratory distress, blindness, pneumonia, pancreatitis, paralysis, brain damage, coma and death by cardiac arrest.

Pesticide labels are severely lacking in important information the consumer needs to know for safety. Most consumers reading "inert ingredients" on labels are usually unaware that the Environmental Protection Agency (EPA) lists *inerts* in four categories (which by the way does not make anyone feel safe):

- Substances known to cause long term health damage and harm the environment.

- Chemicals suspected of damaging health or the environment.

- Chemicals of unknown toxicity.

- Substances of minimal concern.

The EPA has a list of these inert ingredients, although they do not provide a list of products or companies that use potentially harmful or toxic *inert ingredients*.

The Environmental Protection Agency (EPA) Myth: *Most Pesticides Not Tested, Analyzed, Or Approved*

Two important factors should be considered:

1) The EPA "registers" pesticide poisons but the vast majority of these toxic chemicals have never been *"tested"* by the EPA. Often, the EPA must rely on testing data provided by the manufacturing companies themselves (if any has been done at all). It should be noted that the EPA's Pesticide Registration Division is mainly concerned with the "effectiveness" of the insecticides they register. Although the EPA has mandated removal of many dangerous toxic materials, from the marketplace, the consumer still needs to remain aware that the EPA does not provide "approvals" or "analysis" of all ingredients.

2) Any testing of pesticide chemicals required of manufacturers by the EPA uses a 150-pound adult as a measure for the test. This model inappropriately disregards the effect on a person of much lesser weight, such as that of the unborn fetus, small babies, young children and women, or adolescents. The vulnerability of the immune system in the young, old, frail, weak, and sick is not taken into consideration when the testing uses only the 150-pound male as its guideline.

The Grand Rapids Press:
Most Chemicals Not Tested For Toxicity On Humans

Each year 1,500 new chemicals are introduced onto the market. According to the Institute for Children's Environmental Health in Washington, virtually none of the chemicals have been tested by the EPA to discover what impacts may occur when used in "combination" with other chemicals.

Public Broadcasting Service (PBS) "Trade Secrets":
Chemical Body Burden Test Shows Many Poisons

On March 26, 2001, award winning documentary film makers Bill Moyers and Sherry Jones produced an investigative report on toxic chemicals. They revealed that nearly half of the 3,000 high volume chemical products have either never been tested or they've undergone only minimal testing. They also revealed a test for measuring chemical poisons in the body known as **chemical body burdens.** Moyers took the test and learned that his body contained 31 different types of PCB's, 13 different toxins, and pesticides such as malathion, and DDT which had even been banned for years.

Public Broadcasting Service (PBS) "Kids & Chemicals":
Untested Pesticides Cause Childhood Disease

On May 10, 2002, film documentary maker for PBS, Bill Moyers, produced an investigative report on childrens' exposure to chemical toxins including pesticides. He found only about 10 percent of all high volume chemicals had been fully tested for their potential effects on childrens' health and development. As a result, scientists and policy makers are in the dark about the toxicity of thousands of chemicals. The documentary featured Dr. Philip Landrigan, a pioneer in the emerging field of childrens' environmental health from New York's Mount Sinai School of Medicine, who works with scientists around the country to understand how kids are affected by exposure to chemicals.

Dr. Landrigan revealed that over 50 to 60 years ago, most causes of major childrens' illnesses were infectious diseases. Today chronic diseases are the major cause of childrens' illnesses, with asthma now being the leading cause of children being admitted to hospital and missing school. Cancer is the leading killer of children in the United States. It is widely suspected that children exposed to pesticides are at greater risk of childhood cancer. Additionally 5 to 10 percent of all children suffer developmental disabilities such as attention deficit disorder, dyslexia and autism. See the full transcript at: http://www.pbs.org/now/transcript/transcript117_full.html

Micheal J. Fox Foundation:
Pesticides Linked To Parkinson's Disease

An article published June 26, 2006, revealed in the first large-scale, prospective study to examine possible links between chronic, low-dose exposure to pesticides and Parkinson's disease (PD), researchers at the Harvard School of Public Health (HSPH) have shown that individuals reporting exposure to pesticides had a 70 percent higher incidence of PD than those not reporting exposure. No increased risk of PD was found from reported exposure to other occupational hazards, including asbestos, coal or stone dust, chemicals, acids, or solvents.

http://www.michaeljfox.org/news/article.php?id=186

UK Independent:
Government Inquiry—Parkinson's And Pesticides Link

On May 17, 2002, a news report revealed the results of a research study by Stanford University in California. After studying more than 1,000 people, half of whom had Parkinson's, those frequently exposed to pesticides were found to be *twice* as likely to develop the disease.

A Parkinson's specialist, Professor Greenamyre who is on the scientific board of the Michael J Fox Foundation, carried out research in 2000 showing that exposure to pesticides gradually knocked out cells which produce dopamine in the brain by producing highly toxic chemicals called free radicals which are thought to cause cumulative damage to the brain's dopamine system, eventually leading to clinical symptoms.

Dr. Ronald Pearce, a consultant neurologist in charge of studying the brains of victims collected by the Parkinson's Disease Society, said there was a proven link between pesticide exposure and the onset of Parkinson's, and it was time the Government looked at the issue.

UK House Of Commons Agree:
Pesticides Impair Brain Nerves

The main symptoms of long-term poisoning by organophosphate pesticides known as "neuropsychiatric syndrome" (that mimic Parkinson's disease) were discussed at a British Parliamentary hearing. The panel agreed that organophosphate pesticides could impair higher mental functions, which produce several symptoms: mood swings, acute depression, anxiety, memory loss, and cognitive dysfunction, such as mathematical tasks and dealing with life in general. Victims suffer from dizziness, sensory disturbance, neuropathy, language disorders and muscle dysfunction. Intolerance to even very small amounts of alcohol and small traces of the chemicals was noted to cause severe symptoms such as heightened sense of smell, marked decrease in ability to sustain activity and excessive fatigue.

An animal health officer reported terrible side effects on animals that came into contact with organophosphate pesticides to the parliamentary hearing. Animals emerged from pesticide sheep-dips as if they were drunken or intoxicated jumping around uncontrollably on their hind legs. Others couldn't make it out alone and had to be lifted from the sheep-dip.

New York Times:
Toxic Pesticides Cause Brain Plaque And Parkinson's

A May 21st, 2002 report revealed exposure to a pesticide could cause a protein in the brain to misfold forming toxic plaques, which are a suspicious factor contributing to the onset of Parkinson's. Visit the website at: http://www.nytimes.com/2002/05/21/health/21PROT. html?pagewanted=print&position=bottom

Center For Disease Control (CDC):
Pyrethrin And Pyrethroid Side Effects

In a study report titled: *Illnesses Associated With Use of Automatic Insecticide Dispenser Units US, (1986—1999)*, according to the Center for Disease Control (CDC), pyrethrins are insecticides derived from the oleoresin extract of dried chrysanthemum flowers (pyrethrum). Piperonyl butoxide (derived from the sassafras flower) is often added to pyrethrin products to inhibit microsomal enzymes that detoxify pyrethrins.

Although pyrethrins are classified by the EPA as acute toxicity category compounds, they have little systemic toxicity in mammals. However, there are still other health cautions to consider, even with these natural substances. They possess irritant and/or sensitizing properties that can induce contact dermatitis, conjunctivitis, asthma, anaphylactic shock, and gastrointestinal symptoms related to inhalation and cutaneous (skin) exposure to pyrethrin. Resmethrin is a pyrethroid, a class of synthetic insecticides chemically similar to natural pyrethrins. From the 94 pyrethrin/piperonyl butoxide-exposed cases in the combined surveillance data, signs and symptoms for 38 percent involved the eye; 36 percent involved the neurological system; 28 percent involved the respiratory system; 24 percent involved the gastrointestinal system; 21 percent involved the nose and throat; 11 percent involved the skin; and 9 percent involved the cardiovascular system.

Pyrethroids are reported to induce abnormal skin sensation, dizziness, salivation, headache, fatigue, vomiting, diarrhea, irritability to sound and touch, and other central nervous system effects. Some people experienced signs and symptoms in more than one system. Among the three resmethrin-exposed cases, reported signs and symptoms included pruritus, throat irritation, nausea, vomiting, diarrhea, headache, burning sensation in the lungs and a cough. (CDC June 09, 2000) 49(22); 492-5. Website: http://www.cdc.gov/mmwR/preview/mmwrhtml/mm4922a3.htm

Misdiagnosed Pesticide Poisoning Mimics Panic Attacks

A 2001 article by S. Suzanne Fisher reveals anxiety disorders are among the myriad of symptoms found in pesticide poisoning. Pesticides damage acetylcholine, an enzyme in nervous system tissues, preventing its normal breakdown and excretion, thus rendering it unable to do its job. A buildup occurs in the brain that causes over-stimulation of receptor sites in both the central and peripheral nervous systems. One or more symptoms resembling a panic attack can occur such as: tingling or burning hands and feet, feverish or flushed feeling, excessive sweating, blurred vision, dizziness or lightheadedness, a feeling of choking, heart pounding, chest tightness and pains, shortness of breath, nausea, faintness, ringing or buzzing in the ears, or feeling excessively hot or cold. Website: www.naturescountrystore.com/pesticidesandpanicattacks/index.html

A Simple Home Checklist For Child Safety Against Toxic Chemical Pesticides

- Read the labels on all containers stored in your home. Properly dispose of products at your local hazardous waste disposal site, as required.

- Search for places pests enter: Identify and caulk all cracks or crevices where pests may hide and check under doors for gaps. Install door sweeps and weather stripping if necessary.

- Check for leaks, or for water pooling under sinks, around tubs, toilets or any other place. Caulk and fix these areas so pests don't have a ready source of water.

- Properly dispose of products that are unlabeled or illegibly labeled. Never transfer pesticides to unlabeled containers.

- Store pesticides and other chemicals at least four feet off the ground in a locked cabinet.

- Post your local Poison Control Center number near your telephone.

- Teach your children about pesticides and instruct them to stay away.

- Learn about minimum risk pest control methods and use them whenever possible.

Courtesy of Care For Kids Now Campaign

8

Safety Precautions For Diatomaceous Earth (DE)

NOT ALL DIATOMACEOUS EARTH IS EQUAL:

Identifying The Right Kind Of DE For The Right Job

LABELLING LAWS:

What To Look For On The DE Labels

How To Avoid Consumer Confusion

Safety In Moderation

Without proper knowledge or understanding, good things can be abused—just as drinking too much water or taking too many vitamins can be harmful. Like most things in the world, generally the safest rule and best bet is everything should be used or done in moderation. The same principle applies to using food grade Diatomaceous Earth, also known as amorphous non-crystalline silicon dioxide.

Although information in this chapter may seem rather dry, technical, scientific or intellectual, it is helpful to know for gaining confidence in making the switch from poisons to this natural alternative.

Dust Mask & Goggles Recommended To Apply DE

During the application of DE the dust may become airborne. Food grade DE is not a toxin, but as with any kind of dust, even road dust, baby powder or cornstarch, inhaling it can irritate the lungs and it can get into the eyes. Use adequate ventilation and avoid breathing the DE dust. Follow the DE label instructions which should recommend avoiding contact with the eyes by wearing goggles, and also using a dust mask during application. If DE gets in the eyes, immediately flush with water. Remove contacts and flush again. If irritation persists, seek medical attention.

To drastically minimize or entirely eliminate any dust nuisance problem, follow the recipe for making and applying DE as a **liquid solution** *(slurry)* as described in Chapter Six wherever a liquid can be used.

To apply the DE cover the top of novelty applicators such as a colander or sieve to prevent additional DE from rising into the air. Cover or remove electronic equipment that can be damaged by dust. Once the DE settles to the surface upon which it is applied and clears the air, it is no longer an airborne dust nuisance and mask and goggles are no longer needed. Although DE is not a poison, it is drying to the skin and due to the dust irritation, keep children from playing in the DE until the area is cleaned up.

The Vital Importance Of Selection:
Choosing The Right DE For The Right Job

The following is to help you avoid confusion about the various kinds of DE and to identify the correct type or grade of DE for your need. It can't be stressed enough—learning about DE and understanding which one is the right kind for the task, will help you avoid the risks associated with misuse. The right choice of DE and the appropriate grade for the uses in this book is 100 percent **amorphous non-crystalline silicon dioxide** with no additives. Mineral oxides are okay! They are part of the trace minerals found in DE, bound by nature to the silicon dioxide.

This non-toxic type of DE may alternatively be found under other names such as: *amorphous non-crystalline silicon dioxide, Food Codex, Anti-Caking Agent, Inert Carrier, Grain Storage Protectant,* or *Trace Mineral Supplement.* But keep in mind that ingredients other than DE are also lumped under these highly generalized names. Make sure your label says 100 percent Diatomaceous Earth.

Important To Avoid Industrial Grade Crystalline Silica DE

Not all Diatomaceous Earth is equal. There are three classifications or grades of DE:

1) Natural (unheated).

2) Straight calcined (heated).

3) Flux calcined (heated).

Only the natural *unheated DE* is used as *food grade.* The two calcined (heated) grades are not suitable for uses in this book. This industrial grade DE is heated in kilns to extremely high temperatures from 1200 to 1800 degrees Fahrenheit. Heating causes the DE particles to melt together and become crystallized with microscopically sharp needle-like edges that are dangerous to inhale and ingest. Good quality natural unheated DE should be white to off-white in color. The unsuitable calcined grades may be detectable by color. The straight calcined can be pink to light brown, or light yellow to light orange in color, while the flux calcined grade will be harder to distinguish being white to pink or light brown.

There are over 1500 uses for Diatomaceous Earth in the domestic, industrial and agricultural industry requiring it to be processed into different grades and qualities. However, it should be cautioned that the commercial or industrial grade and calcined DE *(crystalline* silica) commonly used in filters for swimming pools, aquariums, juices and beer among hundreds of other products is absolutely NOT SAFE for any uses in food, insecticides or for any other purposes within this book. The use of industrial filtering DE is potentially hazardous to health and should not be used in the home and garden, nor on animals and birds to kill fleas, ticks and lice.

Industrial or commercial grade DE is not registered by the EPA or Department of Agriculture in any state of the United States for the uses in this book. These forms of DE do not meet the FDA food grade criteria and do not meet the GRAS (Generally Recognized As Safe) standard. Industrial or commercial types of DE are also most likely to exceed the crystalline silica safety standards recommended by OSHA (Occupational Safety & Health Administration) 1997, of less than 0.1 percent ($^1/_{10th}$ of 1 percent) *crystalline* silica. In fact, the calcined grades and other types of industrial grade DE contain up to 70 to 80 percent high crystalline silica.

A Caution About Additives In DE

It is important to know The Environmental Protection Agency (EPA) does *not* prohibit additives in DE products. Many DE-based insecticides and grain storage protectants have additives. Any DE that has an additive is not "pure" 100 percent *food grade* amorphous silicon dioxide, so therefore it is not recommended in this book.

It is prudent to read DE labels carefully and check for additives that may also include *inert* (supposedly inactive) ingredients. Additives have been coming under more scrutiny in the last decade or so especially for use in enclosed places. Even some EPA registered DE products containing named natural or synthetic additives such as pyrethrum, pyrethrin or pyrethroid if inhaled can trigger allergic respiratory conditions or diseases such as asthma, which has risen to become the leading cause of childhood diseases today. One preventative measure is to avoid DE with any kind of synthetic or natural additive especially around pregnant and lactating women, babies, small children, chemically sensitive individuals, or anyone with a respiratory or skin ailment, and also puppies and kittens.

Some experts and manufacturers believe a high quality (pure) DE product can be just as effective and competitive as an insecticide without additives. It is believed that some brands of natural DE have a higher number of microscopic lattice-like pores on the surface area of the diatom, which gives the DE more bug killing power due to its higher absorptive and dehydrating capacity without the need for additives.

How To Identify Food Grade DE

Unfortunately, the consumer may become somewhat confused at the lack of availability of food grade DE and further, the identifying information permitted on the DE label. Even when a pure DE product containing only 100 percent amorphous non-crystalline silicon dioxide has met the Food Codex and GRAS (Generally Recognized as Safe) criteria, the following helpful identifying words are *not permitted* by law on the label: *food grade, Food Codex, GRAS, safe, pure, natural, fossilized algae, non-toxic least-toxic,* or *unheated*. The only indication on the label that DE can be used in food may say: *Animal Feed Additive, Anti-Caking Agent, Inert Carrier or Grain Storage Protectant,* or *Trace Mineral Supplement for humans.*

The only EPA-approved phrase that can appear on a home and garden insecticides label is *environmentally friendly, but* oddly, many that qualify do not even say this much. This is too vague, and does not indicate to the consumer if the DE is food grade. Further, environmentally friendly products may even contain natural or synthetic additives which may be hazardous if breathed or ingested, such as the afore-mentioned pyrethrums or pyrethroids.

When the law limits what can be put on a label, consumers can further investigate a specific brand of DE that may interest them by going to the manufacturer's website to check the online label. If it is available, be sure to check the Material Safety Data Sheet (MSDS) where a better description of *Food Codex* may be found.

Although Diatomaceous Earth is sold in a handful of health food stores as a natural *Trace Mineral Supplement*, it does not need to go through the same registration requirements as other DE products, but it is not permitted to make health *claims* on the label, unless the manufacturer has done research and gained FDA approval. It is estimated by one manufacturer of DE that this privilege requires about ten years of research at a cost of about $10 million.

What To Look For On Labels When Buying DE

Until governing agencies provide better clarity by allowing certain identifying words on the label, and until the labeling and registration laws change in the USA, the burden is placed upon the customer who must be knowledgeable and vigilant in discerning which DE product is food grade. For horticultural and agricultural insecticidal purposes including food storage, use the following checklist to get the safest quality DE:

1) Is the name and contact information of the distributor and/or manufacturer on the label? If there is no contact information for the manufacturer or distributor, do not purchase or use.

2) If you wish to use DE in animal feed: The DE should be labeled *Anti-Caking Agent, or Animal Feed Additive, or Inert Carrier.* Note: Although each state's Department of Agriculture registers DE Animal Feed Additive, not all States require that the registration number must appear on the label.

3) If you wish to use DE for storing and protecting grains, seeds, legumes or nuts: To prevent disintegration by weevils and their larvae, or from moisture and mold, the DE used should be labeled *Grain Storage Insecticide* or *Grain Storage Protectant.* There should be an EPA registration number displayed on the label. Farmers use DE in their animal and poultry grain mix formulas as

Anti-Caking Agent or *Animal Feed Additive.* Check with the manufacturer to ensure you are using an appropriate product.

4) If you wish to use DE as an insecticide for the home and garden: Check with the manufacturer or the label to ensure you are using the appropriate DE product and that it is registered. The label should display the word *insecticide.* An EPA registration number (which is issued by each state) should be on the label of all insecticides.

5) Is the product 100 percent Diatomaceous Earth (DE) (amorphous non-crystalline silica?) The uncalcined grade of DE that has been tested by the manufacturer to be very low in crystalline silica content, (less than 0.1 percent) and that does not contain other toxic compounds, is the only type for this consumer. These unheated grades of DE are referred to as natural-milled products because they are merely DE dug from the ground, dried, milled, sized and bagged.

Labels are not required to divulge the amorphous silicon dioxide (non-crystalline) content. However, if it is revealed the highest content is 89 percent. The rest of the content is made up of other pure and naturally-occurring trace minerals (oxides) and moisture already bound by nature with the silicon dioxide, and is regarded as 100 percent pure DE. If you are not sure, and intend to use DE for plants, animals, birds, or in the home and garden, or for agricultural purposes, you can request and check the manufacturer's Material Data Safety Sheet (MSDS) which may be found on their website for a breakdown of minerals.

6) Is the color of the DE off-white or bright white? Do not use pink, yellowish, orange, brown, grey or clay colored DE as it may be a sign of impurities such as clay, ash, iron, mud and other debris, or that it has been heated. When examined and tested in a laboratory, various impurities can be detected. For this reason quality-conscious manufacturers use DE only from specially selected mines known for purity and quality. Whiteness, in some cases, indicates purity, but this is not always the case, as flux calcined (heated)

DE can also be white. In general, whiteness consistently is considered a desirable *cosmetic* feature for marketing purposes. Whiteness also allows DE to be added to another material, such as plastics, and will not adversely change the product's color.

7) Does the DE product contain any additives or inert ingredients? Caution: There should be no added named ingredients or unlisted "inert" ingredients in pure 100 percent *food grade* Diatomaceous Earth. Although food grade Diatomaceous Earth may be labeled as *Inert Carrier* for animal feed, since DE is often used in other products as an inactive ingredient, ironically, in any EPA approved chemical pesticide, other types of *inert ingredients* do not have to be listed individually on the DE product label, even though they may be composed of toxic chemicals suspected as carcinogens or nerve toxins. Manufacturers, being given protection under the umbrella of the "Trade Secrets" law, hide from disclosure the names of inert substances in most chemical pesticides. They are only listed in general as *Inert Ingredients* and give no specific disclosure of their composition.

Inert ingredients, which can make up 1 to 99 percent of a product are used as fillers, binders or activators that can be even more toxic than the prime ingredient, or inerts make the prime ingredient more potent, or they may be added for better adhesiveness. But the adhesive problem with pure DE for use on plants and walls can be solved by the principle of polarity using an electrostatic ionizer to apply DE to the underside of leaves.

The Environmental Protection Agency (EPA): *Issues With The EPA Label Registration*

The EPA is the only federal government agency that registers DE *Insecticide* and *Grain Storage Protectant*. The EPA issues a registration number, which by law must appear on these labels. Note: the EPA only "registers" DE—it does not test DE, nor approve of any DE for different kinds of insecticidal uses. Oddly, the EPA does *not* require submission of data on the crystalline silica content for registering DE as an Insecticide.

The Department of Agriculture
Issues With Registration Of DE

Once the DE *Insecticide* and *Grain Storage Protectant* (which is also an insecticide) are registered with the EPA, they must also be registered with the Department of Agriculture in every state in the United States where the product is intended to be sold. *Anti-Caking Agent* or *Animal Feed Additive,* is registered by each Department of Agriculture and not the EPA. However, the registration information by this department is *not permitted* on the label. Manufacturers receive a registration certificate from the state's Department of Agriculture, which does *not* test DE intended for animal or poultry use.

DE Not Required By FDA To Meet 1997 Occupational Safety & Health Administration (OSHA) Guideline

Contrary to what is popularly thought, the Food and Drug Administration (FDA) and OSHA do not *certify, register or test* any form of DE, even if the product has met the FDA food grade or **GRAS (Generally Recognized As Safe)** criteria.

It is *not mandatory* for DE to meet the FDA standards of GRAS, food grade, or **Food Codex.** Surprisingly, it is also *not mandatory* for the *crystalline* silica content of any kind of DE for any purpose to meet the 1997 OSHA recommendation of less than 0.1 percent. Trace mineral supplements for human ingestion, are not required to be registered by either the FDA or the EPA if the label does not make a health benefit *claim.*

Some manufacturers have voluntarily proven through laboratory analysis (although *not* mandatory) that the quality of their DE meets the FDA's food grade or OSHA's 1997 crystalline silica recommendation or standard. Manufacturers wishing to prove the superior safety and quality of their DE to inquiring customers are usually more than willing to provide documentation on their website of the laboratory analysis, and a Material Safety Data Sheet (MSDS) which reveals this information.

What To Look For On The Material Safety Data Sheet

The Material Safety Data Sheet (MSDS) contains useful information to help you with your research on finding the highest quality DE as it displays the chemical identity of Diatomaceous Earth. A lot of the information seen on the MSDS may appear too technical and not make any sense if you are not familiar with chemistry. However, if you are looking for the best and highest quality DE, you will want to check at least two things—the more hazardous *crystalline silica* content, and the safer *non-crystalline silicon dioxide* (amorphous) content.

The best and highest quality DE has between 86-89 percent *non-crystalline* (amorphous) silicon dioxide. In contrast, of most concern is the amount of the *crystalline* silica, which should be very low—the lower the level the better, at 0.1 percent or less ($^1/_{10th}$ of 1 percent) which should not to be confused with 1.0 percent. This level was established by the 1997 OSHA recommendation. Although the OSHA standard is not mandatory for any DE purpose, it is a safety guideline for which some manufacturers qualify, and it can be shown on their MSDS.

Although the crystalline silica content of the DE is submitted on the MSDS when applying for registration to the above government or state agencies, registration is *not* declined if the crystalline silica content is above the OSHA's 0.1 percent guideline!

An MSDS can be obtained from the manufacturer upon request, or from their website. If you request an MSDS and do not receive one, plus if the crystalline silica content is not on the label of the product you want to purchase, DO NOT USE that brand of DE.

Know The Health Hazards Of Industrial Grade DE

Crystalline silica occurs to varying extents in all Diatomaceous Earth. Some companies have a very low content, while other sources of have more. Thermal treatment of DE by the industry to make many types of commercial products creates even more crystalline silica in the DE.

The hazards of high crystalline silica and the commercial or industrial uses for this grade of Diatomaceous Earth (DE) are mentioned below, not just as a sideline of interest, but also to help you identify the right kind of DE. The manufacture's intended end-use is a means the consumer must use for distinguishing the safer *food grade* DE from industrial grade DE. For example, do not use an aquarium or pool filter DE as an insecticide. This type of DE can poison pets if used for fleas as it may also contain additional toxic chemicals.

The following are further reasons why you should not use industrial grade DE for home, garden, animal and bird insecticidal use. High *crystalline silica* industrial grade DE has been kiln fired and (calcined) at over 1,700° F, partially melting the mineral and increasing the *crystalline silica* content to over 70 percent. In contrast the author recommends following the OSHA 1997 guidelines and using DE with only 0.1 ($^1/_{10th}$ of 1 percent) or less.

Typically fresh water DE has a significantly lower amount of crystalline silica than salt water sources, which are naturally higher in crystalline silica to begin with. However, "natural-grade" freshwater DE's can also contain a higher crystalline silica than the OSHA limit. If fresh water DE is highly heated, it will also convert to the more hazardous high crystalline silica just as salt water DE does. Any kind of highly heated *calcined* DE is potentially *toxic*.

Microscopic sized particles of the calcined DE become solidified like glass, which are hazardous to human or animal health if inhaled or ingested. A lung disease called silicosis can result from breathing in the tiny sized particles of crystalline silica. The needle-like microscopic chips are capable of lodging in the lung tissue causing calcification, a type of pulmonary fibrosis, emphysema and respiratory impairment—the oldest known occupational lung disease, which does the same damage as that caused by asbestos. Tunnel drillers and workers have suffered this disease, and fossil preparers in labs get it from breathing sand blasted and matrix dust that is released through preparation.

The Merck Medical Journal states that silicosis can become apparent in less than 10 years after inhalation exposures, although it can take up to 30 years to manifest. This disease is largely preventable. Proper and conscientious use of masks, effective dust extractors, and adequate ventilation helps to prevent silicosis. If crystalline silica exceeding 0.1 percent is *ingested*, it has been known to cause cancer of the intestines and liver, and also uroliths, which are stones in the kidneys or urinary tract.

The more abrasive industrial grade *crystalline silica* DE is used for swimming pools or fish tank filtration systems, and is commonly found in most hardware or nursery stores. Unsuspecting consumers will be encouraged to buy industrial grade DE, yet 100 percent amorphous unheated DE will do the job. Look for a DE *Animal Feed Additive* or *Anti-Caking Agent,* jot down the manufacturer's information, contact them and request an MSDS. It would behoove you to know that industrial grade DE is also used in sandblasting, soap, pottery, ceramics, fire retardants, deodorizers, kitty litter, cosmetics, abrasive cleaners, metal polishers, paper, auto polish compounds, cement additives, construction insulation, toothpaste, synthetic jewelry (such as turquoise and terrazzo), road materials, industrial oil and toxic chemical spill containment, paint, flatteners, texturizers, and clarifying filters for beer, wine, juices, honey, and syrup.

Going Green Through The Gray Areas of "Red Tape"

Due to the above government labeling restrictions and cautionary anomalies, consumers seriously looking for a non-toxic or least-toxic insecticide such as DE, find it difficult to discriminate between pure non-toxic food grade DE and a poison, even when the two containers are standing right next to each other! Interestingly though, unlike toxic insecticides, the EPA does not require that DE insecticides be sold in "child proof" containers.

This complicated problem is of huge concern when the majority of people don't know exactly what Diatomaceous Earth is. The author witnessed a mother holding her baby while choosing a can of pesticide poison over a DE insecticide because the anomalies and inadequacies in labeling laws do not help consumers in identifying and distinguishing what is truly safe, pure and natural, or what is potentially a deadly poison. The current restrictions that these laws pose are in themselves a potential risk to human health.

Unfortunately, it is scary to know that misled consumers who buy chemical poisons and leave a pure non-toxic *food grade* DE product on the shelf because they cannot tell the difference due to these labeling restrictions are people who are at the highest risk of unintentionally harming others with a poisonous product (i.e., couples planning a family, pregnant and lactating women, parents of small children, caregivers, pet owners and home owners). Home is one place where we all want to know we are safe from poisons.

Conclusion: To the EPA's credit, it continues to remove certain poisons from the market. However, even though they register many more new products, these untested and toxic chemicals replace the few that are withdrawn. A growing number of consumers are proving they really prefer to be steered towards safer alternatives. A fully informative label is the first step in the disclosure process of identifying safer products such as DE, but for now the consumer is required to do a bit more of their own homework and contact the manufacturer or distributor due to these label omissions and restrictions.

Still, pure non-toxic food grade Diatomaceous Earth is a far safer alternative than any synthetic toxic chemical for your health and the health of your family. DE is here to stay, and in the future will become better researched, gain more public acceptance, and will be more frequently used in the rapidly evolving *green* era. Food grade DE certainly has the potential to become a common household name, given the safety factors compared to toxic chemicals. DE is also here to stay in another way. As long as it stays dry in storage or where applied, and as long as it remains undisturbed, it will remain effective as a safer insecticide and last indefinitely.

This book will help you solve a multitude of questions about things that bug you, and help you know what to do to allay any hesitancy about switching to natural-milled, food grade Diatomaceous Earth, from dangerous chemical toxins. Good health to you and your family, and to the millions of animals and birds that share our world.

Sources Of Reference Materials

INDIVIDUAL EXPERTS

ARTICLES & BOOKS

JOURNALS & NEWS SERVICES

**HEALTH RESEARCH & EDUCATIONAL
FOUNDATIONS, NETWORKS & ORGANIZATIONS**

TELEVISION DOCUMENTARIES

GOVERNING & REGULATING AGENCIES

INDIVIDUAL EXPERTS

Dr. Bh. Subramanyam, Ph.D., Entomology, Department of Grain Sciences, Kansas State University, Manhattan, Kansas. provided verbal information on the amount of Diatomaceous Earth to apply to ground flours and whole grains. Co-editor with David W. Hagstrum of the text book *Alternatives to Pesticides in Stored-Product IPM,* Chapter 12 on *Inert Dusts* which describe the "mode of action" of Diatomaceous Earth as a desiccant (dehydrating substance).

Dr. Bart Dees: Department of Entomology, Texas A&M University, College Station, TX.

R. Blake Dobbins, Spectrum Electrostatic Sprayers, Inc., provided information on the benefits and efficiency of using electrostatic sprayers to apply DE for adhesiveness in small gardens to large acreage, including aerial coverage. Houston, TX. Visit Website: www.spectrumsprayer.com

Richard Breese and Frederick M. Bodycomb: Co-editors of two publications above and preeminent sources of reference material in the professional world of minerals and mineral deposits, worldwide. They provide a comprehensive background of this amazing mineral's geologic and commercial/industrial history. They also provide a current list of commercial producers of Diatomaceous Earth (described as Diatomite in industrial uses). Richard Breese (Geologist) contributed to comments on the geology, mineralogy, and commercial nomenclature of Diatomaceous Earth for this book. Breese Geologic Consulting, POB 524, Lyons, Colorado, 80540.

Richard Evons: Provided valuable information on many aspects of Diatomaceous Earth (DE) including the different qualities of DE, cautions and government standards of OSHA, EPA, FDA, USDA, and information on the Material Safety Date Sheet (MSDS) regarding crystalline silica content etc. P.O. Box 7801, Boise, ID 83707.

Wally Tharp: *Interview with Wally Tharp: Acres USA* magazine. Wally Tharp provided some history, and uses of DE, and many of the anecdotal comments from several people he knows as successful users of DE, and information on some of the tools and applicators for applying DE. 3434B Vassar NE, Albuquerque, NM 87107.

Steve Tvedten: Expert consultant on safer alternatives contributed to the chapter on health risks linked to toxic chemical pesticides.
Email: steve@getipm.com
Website: http://www.thebestcontrol2.com

Dr. Robert VanderMeer, USDA.

ARTICLES & BOOKS

A Back To The Future Product: by David Pittman. In his research on the immune system Pittman found people with chronic diseases have weak immune systems, digestive system problems, toxic deposits accumulating somewhere in the body, parasites and other microbes such as bacteria, fungus, or viruses which can live part-time or long-term within the body. Diatomaceous Earth can relieve the body of parasites and microbes in the digestive tract and colon and so improve health. (Oct, 1999).

Adverse Health Effects Of Pesticide Endocrine Disruptor Hormones: In a 1998 report, the World Health Organization revealed that natural and synthetic endocrine disruptor hormones are substances originating outside the body such as pesticides that alter functions of the endocrine system, with resulting adverse health effects including in the offspring. These hormones also accumulate in water sources. Some of the effects have been observed in studies of invertebrates, fish, amphibia, reptiles, birds and mammals. The following potential human health effects are a guide to the suggested risk posed by endocrine disruptors. Cancers of the breast, prostate and testes; male infertility due to reduced quantity and quality of semen; impaired behavioral and mental function in children; impaired function of the immune system and thyroid particularly in children. http://www.who.int/water_sanitation_health/industrypollution/en/index2.html

Animals Parasitic In Man: by Geoffrey Lapage. A medical book that reveals no organ in the body is immune from parasites. Dover Publications (1957).

Are You Clear Of Parasites? by Dr. Ross Anderson, N. D. An article on parasites being everywhere—a major health problem. (1996).

Cancer: It's A Growth Industry: David Ross reported the incidence of cancer now strikes nearly one in every two men, and over one in every three women in their lifetimes. Dr. Samuel Epstein, professor emeritus of environmental medicine at the University of Illinois School of Public Health, and Chairman of the Cancer Prevention Coalition (CPC), predicted by the year 2050 the growth rate of cancer will have doubled. *http://www.preventcancer.com/publications/pdf/Interview percent 20 percent 20Jun percent 2003.html*

Childhood Leukemia And Parents' Occupational And Home Exposure: Lowengart, R.A., et al. 1987. J. Nat. Cancer Inst. 79 (1):39-46.

Common-Sense Pest Control: by W. Olkowski, S. Daar, and H. Olkowski—*Least-Toxic Solutions for Your Home, Garden, Pets and Community.* (1991). The Taunton Press, Newtown, CT. 715pp. www.epa.gov/pesticides/ipm/schoolipm/recread.pdf

Diatomaceous Earth (DE) Lowers Blood Cholesterol Concentrations: by H. Wachter, M. Lechleitner, E. Artner-Dworzak, A. Hausen, E. Jarosch, B. Widner, J. Patsch, K . Pfeiffe, D. Fuchs—A twelve week Austrian study on DE at the Institute of Medical Chemistry and Biochemistry, University of Innsbruck, Austria.

Designer Poisons: How To Protect Your Health And Home From Toxic Pesticides: by Marion Moses, M.D., a highly respected medical doctor and scientist experienced in environmental and occupational medicine, and foremost authority on the devastating effects of chronic exposures to common household pesticides, which tragically result in cancer, reproductive disorders, and damage to the brain and nervous system. All children have been exposed in the womb if either parent has been exposed to toxic chemicals during the pregnancy, which can disrupt healthy development and later sexual functioning. One study suggested that lawn sprays can cause a four-fold increase of cancer in children. This book is strongly recommended for physicians, toxicologists, occupational medicine clinics, public health officials, health and safety regulation administrators, attorneys and anyone interested in the diagnosis, etiology and prevention of chronic chemical exposure, injuries and illnesses. (1995) Pesticide Education Center, Ph. 415-391-8511, 800-732-3733. e-mail: pec@igc.apc.aorg Website: www.pesticides.org/educmaterials.html

Evaluating DE, Silicon Aerogel Dusts To Protect Stored Wheat From Insects: USDA, Market Research Report #1038. (1975).

Exposures And Other Agricultural Risk Factors For Leukemia Among Men In Iowa And Minnesota: by Brown, L.M. et al. Cancer Res. 50:6585-6591. (1990).

Family Pesticide Use In The Home, Garden, Orchard, And Yard: by J. R. Davis, R. C. Brownson, and R. Garcia. Arch. Environ. Contam., Toxicol., 22:260-266. (1992).

Fatality Associated With Inhalation Of A Pyrethrin Shampoo: by P. M. Wax, and R. S. Hoffman. Clin. Toxicol. 32(4):457-460. (1994).

Fire Ant Control: Natural Food and Farming, (July/August 1993).

Green, Thrifty & Safer Home Solutions: *1001 Easier, Faster, Healthier & More Resourceful Everyday Household Tips and Tricks,* by Tui Rose R.N.—A healthful tips practical guide for cleaning, laundry, stain removal, new uses for old stuff, grannies old wisdom, and alternatives to toxic chemicals including pesticides. Contains a chapter on how to use Diatomaceous Earth in the home and garden. 250 pp. Website: http://www.TuiRoseTips.com

Handbook Of Pesticide Toxicology: by W. J. Hayes and E. R. Laws—Defines manifestations and diagnosis of acute pyrethroid poisoning. Vol 2. San Diego, California: Academic Press, Inc., (1991). (Reference printed in CDC June 09, 2000) 49(22);492-5).

Home Pesticide Use And Childhood Cancer—*A Case-Control Study,* by J. K. Leiss and D. A. Savitz. Amer. J. Public Health 85(2):249-252. (1995).

Immune System Care And Feeding: *Galen Knight Ph.D.,* Vitale Therapeutics, Inc. offers suggestions for how to detoxify the body in many ways, including using Diatomaceous Earth. www.vitaletherapeutics.org

Industrial Minerals And Rocks (7th Edition): *A Chapter on Diatomite,* by Richard O. Y. Breese and Frederick M. Bodycomb. Breese Geologic Consulting, P.O. Box 524, Lyons, Colorado, 80540.

Inert Pesticide Ingredients Can Be More Toxic Than The Primary Ingredient: Mention of inert ingredients being potentially toxic was found online at: World Water Day 2001: Pollution from industry, mining and agriculture. www.who.int/water_sanitation_health/industrypollution/en/index2.html

Journal Of Parasitic Disease: The Indian Society for Parasitology, Volume 27, #2, 2003 includes mention of *Animals Parasitic in Man* by Geoffrey Lapage.
http://parasitologyindia.org/journal_content/Vol percent 2027 percent 20No percent 202 percent 20December.pdf

Journal Of Parasitology: *How much human helminthiasis is there in the world?* by Dr. D. W. T. Crompton, 85:379-403 (1999).

Globe And Mail: *Pesticides Laced With Unlabelled Substances,* by Martin Mittelstaedt—Pesticide manufacturers are required only to identify the "active" ingredients on their product labels with little or no disclosure for "inert" ingredients. (June 9, 2001). http://www.theglobeandmail.com/

Medical Parasitology: by E. K. Markell and M. Voge—Therapy to remove entire tapeworms from the small intestine is only successful if the whole worm is expelled. If the head remains, the entire worm will grow back. Saunders, Philadelphia, (1981).

Mining Engineering: *Diatomite,* by Richard O. Y. Breese, (June 1999), Breese Geologic Consulting, P.O.B. 524, Lyons, Colorado, 80540.

Mother Nature's Bug Killer: by Anthony De Crosta, Organic Gardening, (June 1979).

Pesticides And Panic Attacks: *Pesticide Symptoms Mimic Those of Panic Attacks Causing Frequent Misdiagnoses!* by S. Suzanne Fisher—Pesticides damage acetylcholine, an enzyme in nervous system tissues, resulting in accumulation and over stimulation in the nervous systems. (2001).

Potential Exposure And Health Risks Of Infants Following Indoor Residential Pesticide Applications: by R. A. Fenske, et al. Amer. J. Public Health 80 (6):689-693. (1990).

Pyrethrins Pesticide Information Profile: Extension Toxicology Network (EXTOXNET). (March 1994).

Pyrethrin Poisoning From Commercial-Strength Flea And Tick Spray: by D. L. Paton, and J. S. Walker. Amer. J. Emerg Med (1988); 6:232--5. (Reference printed in CDC June 09, 2000) 49(22):492-5).

Risk Factors For Brain Tumors In Children: by E. Gold, et al. 1979. Amer. J. Epidemiol. 109(3):309-319.

Teratogenicity Study On Pyrethrins And Rotenone (Of Natural Origin) And Ronnel In Pregnant Rats: by K. R. Khera, C. Whalen, and G. Angers. Teratol. 23(2):45A-46A. (Abst). (1981). http://www.pesticide.org/factsheets.html

The Organic Manual, & Texas Organic Gardening Book: by Howard Garrett, author and columnist for Acres Magazine and guest radio speaker on WBAP (The Natural Way). P. O. Box 140650, Dallas, TX 75214.

Tired Or Toxic: by Dr. Sherry Rogers, M. D., who is a Diplomat of the American Board of Family Practice, a Fellow of the American College of Allergy and Immunology and a Diplomat of the American Academy of Environmental Medicine. She is a lecturer of yearly original scientific material, as well as advanced courses for physicians. Dr. Rogers is also author of several other health and environmentally related books—among the many are: *Detoxify Or Die, The E.I. Syndrome, Wellness Against All Odds, The Scientific Basis For Selected Environmental Medicine Techniques, and Chemical Sensitivity.* "We are the first generation to be exposed to an unprecedented number of chemicals." Detoxifying these in the body causes serious deficiencies which results in chronic disease. Like canaries used in mines to warn miners of the presence of dangerous gases, Dr. Rogers says Multiple Chemical Sensitivity sufferers warn everyone that certain substances including chemical pesticides are toxic for everyone. Dr. Rogers describes the mechanism, diagnosis and treatment complete with scientific references of chemical sensitivity, and other diseases including chronic candidiasis and cancer. 400 pp. Prestige Publishing P.O.Box 3068 Syracuse, NY 13220. Ph. 1-800-846-6687.
E-Mail: orders@prestigepublishing.com
Website: www.prestigepublishing.com

Urinary Silicon Excreted By Rats Following Oral Administration Of Silicon Compound: by G. M. Benke, and T. W. Osborn. Food Cosmet. Toxicol. 17:123-127. (1978).

Worming Without Chemicals: by Jean Winter, The New Farm, (January 1982).

JOURNALS & NEWS SERVICES

Consumer Reports: Getting the Bugs Out—How to Control Household Pests: (July 1993).

Dallas Morning News: House and Gardens the Natural Way, (May 28, 1993).

Discover Magazine: An article on clinical trials in Canada using Diatomaceous Earth to treat children infected with toxic *E.coli.* (November 22, 1994).

Environmental Science And Technology: *Study Finds Toxic Soup In Household Air And Dust*—A study by environmental toxicology scientists for the Silent Spring Institute found alarming levels of chemicals and endocrine-disruptor pesticides including some that were banned over ten years ago—most homes exceeded the EPA's guidelines.

National Geographic Magazine: *Those Marvelous Myriad Diatoms,* by Richard D. Hoover, diatom explorer and microscopist. (June 1979).

National Post: *Pesticide Poisoning Passes To Grandchildren,* by Veronique Mandal—A researcher of The Ontario College of Family Physicians, Dr. Margaret Sanborn, found even extremely low levels of pesticide poisons seriously affect the genetics of children. (April 24, 2004).

New Scientist: *Carpets Harbor Toxic Dust:* Environmental engineer John Roberts reveals household carpet dust contains high levels of chemical contaminants including pesticides that are tracked inside the home on footwear. (May, 2001).

Newsweek: *What's Killing the Frogs?* Fred Guterl reported that frogs warn us about the implications on animal and human health caused by dangerous chemical pesticides just as canaries warn coal miners of lethal gases. Scientists for both U.S. Geological Survey and University of California, Berkeley found frogs and tadpoles were born with leg and genital deformities. *(May 13, 2002).*

New York Times: *Parkinson's:* Exposure to pesticides are a suspicious factor for causing a protein in the brain to misfold forming toxic plaques, which contributing to the onset of Parkinson's. (May 21st, 2002). http://www.nytimes.com/2002/05/21/health/21PROT. html?pagewanted=print&position=bottom

PANUPS (Pesticide Action Network Updates Service): *New Reports Find Pesticides in People:* Research shows low levels of chemical pesticide exposure to the fetus or young children can cause irreversible damage. (February 14, 2003).
http://www.cdc.gov/exposurereport/

PANUPS: Evidence shows that children who eat more organic food have fewer chemicals in their bodies. (August 2, 2002). http://www.panna.org/resources/panups/panup_20020802. dv.html

Pesticide Action Network: *School Governor Suffers Numbness After Head Lice Treatment:* A school principal used a medically recommended head lice treatment and suffered a numb torso and arms diagnosed by Dr. Sarah Myhill as peripheral neuropathy. http://www.panna.org

Pesticide Action Network Pesticide Database: Provides pesticide information from many different sources. Includes definitions, references and user manual. www.pesticideinfo.org

PR Newswire: *Vets Wage War on Fleas Naturally:* (June 28, 1994).

The Grand Rapids Press: *Federal Study To Measure Pollution In People:* Babies have detectable levels of poisons in their blood streams from birth. By adulthood we have accumulated a scientific estimate of at least 500 chemicals in our bodies! (March 22, 2001).

The Hamilton Spectator: *Cut Pesticide Use—Doctors Warn of Links to Deadly Diseases, but Findings Disputed by Chemical Industry Group:* Suzanne Morrison reports Ontario family doctors urge limiting the use of common pesticides after a major study strongly linked pesticides to deadly diseases. (April 24, 2004).

Scottish Scientists Link Certain Pesticides To Childhood Leukemia: A study found that pregnant women, who were exposed to certain pesticides, were *ten times* more likely to have a baby with leukemia.
http://scotlandonsunday.com/news.cfm?id=SS01013063&feed=N

UK Independent: *Government Orders An Inquiry Into Pesticide Links To Parkinson's Disease:* A Stanford University, California research study by a Parkinson's specialist Professor Greenamyre, scientific board member of the Michael J Fox Foundation discovered those frequently exposed to pesticides were twice as likely to develop Parkinson's disease. Pesticides knocked out cells which produce dopamine in the brain. May 17, 2002.

A Cancer Journal: An International journal of the American Cancer Society for clinicians published a study of children which revealed exposure to household insecticides increased the likelihood of Non-Hodgkins Lymphoma by three to seven times and increased the risk of Lymphoblastic Lymphoma by 12.5 times. (December 1, 2000). Published for the American Cancer Society by Lippincott Williams and Wilkins. www.cancer.org/docroot/PUB/content
Cited by **UniSci Daily University Science,** http://unisci.com/

Wall Street Journal: *More States Cracking Down on Use of Home Pesticides,* June Fletcher, (1996).

Wikipedia: *The Free Online Encyclopedia—Diatomaceous Earth Files:* http://en.wikipedia.org/wiki/diatomaceous_earth

HEALTH RESEARCH & EDUCATIONAL FOUNDATIONS, NETWORKS & ORGANIZATION

B.I.R.C. (Bio-Integral Resource Center): Distributors of the book, *Common Sense Pest Control,* P. O. Box 7414, Berkeley, CA 94707, 510-524-2567.

Cancer Prevention Coalition: CPC was founded in 1994, by **Dr. Samuel S. Epstein, M. D.,** professor at the University of Illinois, Chicago School of Public Health where he serves as Professor Emeritus of Environmental and Occupational Medicine. He is also Chairman of the Cancer Prevention Coalition. Dr Epstein is also an internationally recognized authority on the causes and prevention of cancer, and has published some 270 scientific articles and 11 books, including the prize-winning *The Politics of Cancer (1978), The Safe Shopper's Bible (1995), The Breast Cancer Prevention Program, The Politics of Cancer Revisited (1998), Mutagenicity of Pesticides, Hazardous Wastes in America, Cancer in Britain, Unreasonable Risk, How to avoid cancer from per-sonal care and cosmetic products, Cancer Gate-How to Win the Losing Cancer War, What's In your Milk (2006)* to name just a few. In 2005 Dr. Samuel Epstein, M.D., received the Albert Schweitzer World Academy of medicine Golden Grand Medal for humanitarianism for his longstand-ing and pioneering international contributions to cancer prevention. University of Illinois at Chicago, School of Public Health, MC 922, 2121 West Taylor Street, Chicago, IL 60612, Ph. 312-996-2297.
Dr. Epstein's Website: http://www.preventcancer.com

CHEC (Children's Health Environmental Coalition): CHEC is a national non-profit organization dedicated to educating the public, specifically parents and caregivers, about environmental toxins that threaten children's health, through scientific research data and changing government policies to protect children. CHEC's 1994 study, *Handle With Care: Children and Environmental Carcinogens,* inspired action to change current environmental protection policy. In March 1995, Senator Boxer proposed an amendment to the "Toxic

Substances Control Act", entitled: *The Children's Environmental Protection Act (CEPA),* which was designed to address the need for greater protections for children, as well as for other vulnerable groups including pregnant women and the elderly. CHEC also released a report, *The State of Children's Health and Environment,* 2002, containing commonsense solutions for parents and policymakers, which can be downloaded from the website. CHEC also released an educational video entitled: *Not Under My Roof: Protecting Your Baby From Toxins At Home,* which stresses the importance of creating a toxin-free home and demonstrates how to do so, featuring Kelly Preston and Olivia Newton-John.

CHEC's Healthe House: is an interactive source information on environmental health risks children face in the home. By taking a virtual tour through the rooms of a typical house, visitors can learn how to make their own homes safer. Visitors to the website will find out how to sign up for the First Steps program, a monthly, personalized email program designed to offer timely information to minimize a fetus' or baby's exposure to toxic chemicals. By registering the due date or birth date of a child, tailored information corresponding to the stage of development is sent. 12300 Wilshire Blvd. Suite 320, Los Angeles, CA 90025. Ph. 310-820-2030. Website: www.checnet.org

Center For Disease Control: A report including the study of side effects from natural or synthetic pyrethrins and piperonyl butoxide (PBO). In a study report entitled: *Illnesses Associated With Use of Automatic Insecticide Dispenser Units US, (1986—1999),* according to the Center for Disease Control (CDC), even natural pyrethrin insecticides derived from the dried chrysanthemum flowers (pyrethrum), with added piperonyl butoxide (derived from the sassafras flower) can be toxic to health causing asthma and many other symptoms including anaphylactic shock, particularly in children and the elderly. CDC, (June 09, 2000) 49(22);492-5).

Mercola Optimal Wellness Center: *Agricultural Pesticides Linked To Miscarriage,* by Dr. Joseph Mercola, author of a free newsletter on natural health and medical news. Mothers who live within 1-square mile of areas sprayed with poisonous pesticides may have more miscarriages and babies born with birth defects. (Feb, 28, 2001). http://www.mercola.com

The Micheal J. Fox Foundation: The Michael J. Fox Foundation for Parkinson's Research is dedicated to ensuring the development of a cure for Parkinson's disease within this decade through an aggressively funded research agenda. Actor Michael J. Fox established the Foundation in May 2000 shortly after announcing his retirement from the ABC television show Spin City. In 1998 he publicly disclosed that he had been diagnosed with young-onset Parkinson's disease seven years earlier.

A June 26, 2006 article entitled: *Pesticide Exposure Associated With Parkinson's Disease* revealed: In the first large-scale, prospective study to examine possible links between chronic, low-dose exposure to pesticides and Parkinson's disease (PD), researchers at the Harvard School of Public Health (HSPH) have shown that individuals reporting exposure to pesticides had a 70 percent higher incidence of PD than those not reporting exposure. No increased risk of PD was found from reported exposure to other occupational hazards, including asbestos, coal or stone dust, chemicals, acids, or solvents. The Michael J. Fox Foundation for Parkinson's Research Grand Central Station, P.O. Box 4777, New York, NY 10163. Ph. 1-800-708-7644, Website: http://www.michaeljfox.org/news/article.php?id=186

National Poison Prevention Week Council: The national toll-free phone number for poison-control centers is 1-800-222-1222. A checklist is available at website: http://www.cpsc.gov/cpscpub/pubs/383.html

PANNA (Pesticide Action Network North America): A non-profit networking organization working to replace more than $35 billion a year in pesticide use with safer alternatives. They link local and international consumers, labor, health, environment and agriculture groups into an international citizens' action network. The other four PAN Regional Centers include PAN Africa, PAN Asia/ Pacific, PAN Europe and PAN Latin America. Phone 415-981-1771. Email panna@panna.org Websites: http://www.panna.org or http://www.pan-international.org/

The Pesticide Education Center (PEC): A non-profit organization founded in 1988 to educate workers and the public about the hazards of pesticides to human health and the environment. PEC provides critical information on health effects and safer alternative pest control methods to the public to educate consumers to make more informed choices to protect themselves, their families, their pets, their neighbors, and the environment from toxic pesticides. The founder and president of the PEC, Dr. Marion Moses, is a physician specializing in occupational and environmental medicine with many years experience investigating and diagnosing pesticide-related illnesses. She is the author of *Designer Poisons*. The center produces videos and publishes books and other materials. Pesticide Education Center, P.O. Box 225279, San Francisco, CA .94122-5279. Ph. 415-665-4722, Fax 415-665-2693, email: pec@igc.org Website: www.pesticides.org/educmaterials.html

Silent Spring Institute: SSI is named after the trend-setting 1960 book entitled *Silent Spring,* of renowned biologist and environmentalist Rachel Carson, who died from breast cancer at the age of 56. Silent Spring Institute is a non-profit research organization dedicated to researching, identifying and changing the links between the environment (including pesticides) and women's health, especially breast cancer. The Institute connects local residents, community groups, regulatory agencies, scientists, toxicologists, physicians, public health and environmental organizations across the country to promote sharing of information. SSI was honored by the EPA (U.S. Environmental Protection Agency) in 2000 with an Environmental Merit Award. Newton, MA. (617) 332-4288. Website: www.silentspring.org

The Lymphoma Foundation Of America: *Do Pesticides Cause Lymphoma?* The LFA reveals 117 scientific research studies worldwide link pesticides to a current "epidemic" of lymphoma, the second fastest rising cancer in the US. When pesticides are used inside the home, lymphoma rates in children are higher. (May, 2001). Website: www.lymphomaresearch.org

TELEVISION DOCUMENTARIES

PBS Now: *Kids And Chemicals:* An investigative documentary by Bill Moyers produced a report on children's health after exposure to chemical toxins including pesticides. (May 10, 2002). http://www.pbs.org/now/transcript/transcript117_full.html

PBS: *Trade Secrets:* An investigative documentary produced by Bill Moyers and Sherry Jones reveals nearly half of the 3,000 high volume chemical products have never been tested. They also revealed a test for measuring chemical poisons in the body known as *chemical body burdens*. (March 26, 2001).

The Discovery Health Channel: *Toxic Legacies—Examining The Endocrine Question:* Chemical toxins known as endocrine disruptors become trapped in our fatty tissues, which causes our own hormone signals to be disrupted. http://health.discovery.com/premiers/toxic/inside.html

GOVERNING & REGULATING AGENCIES

Center For Disease Control: *Illnesses Associated With Use Of Automatic Insecticide Dispenser Units US, (1986—1999.)* A study report on the side effects of pyrethrins and piperonyl butoxide (PBO).

EPA Federal Register: *Reclassification Of Certain Inert Ingredients:* Federal Register: March 8, 2002 (Volume 67, Number 46). Eight inert ingredients have been determined to be animal carcinogens, thus meeting one of the criteria for reclassification from "Potentially Toxic Inerts/High Priority for Testing" to List 1 "Inerts of Toxicological Concern." EPA also intends to reclassify

the inert ingredient, Rhodamine B, from List 1 to List 4B, "Inerts for which EPA has sufficient information to reasonably conclude that the current use pattern in pesticide products will not adversely affect public health or the environment." Visit Websites:
www.epa.gov/fedrgstr/EPA-PEST/2002/March/Day-08/p5445.htm
www.epa.gov/opprd001/inerts/fr54.htm

Food And Drug Administration (FDA) *Federal Register 1961 And 1981:* Rules and Regulations, Title 21, Chapter 1, Subheading 120.188, Exemption of food grade Diatomaceous Earth (Anti-Caking Agent and Grain Storage Protectant) from "tolerance" requirements to protect stored barley, buckwheat, corn, oats, rice, rye, pea sorghum (milo) and wheat.

Food And Drug Administration (FDA): Food Grade Criteria (as of 4/1/06). Visit Website: http://a257.g.akamaitech. net/7/257/2422/10apr20061500/edocket.access.gpo.gov/ cfr_2006/aprqtr/pdf/21cfr573.320.pdf#search=percent_2221percent 20CFR percent 20Chapter percent 201 percent 2053.340percent 20percent 20diatomaceous percent 20OR percent 20earthpercent 20_percent 22Food percent 20and percent 20Drug percent20Administration percent 20HHS percent 22 percent 22

International Agency For Research on Cancer (IARC): *Monographs On The Evaluation Of Carcinogenic Risks To Humans (Silica)*, Volume 68, (05/20/97) p. 41, Summary of Data Reported and Evaluations (5.1-5.1): IARC is a division of the United Nations World Health Organization (WHO). IARC mission is to coordinate and conduct research on the causes of human cancer, the mechanisms of carcinogenesis, and to develop scientific strategies for cancer control. The Agency is involved in both epidemiological and laboratory research. They critically review data from medical and epidemiological studies, and disseminate scientific information through publications, meetings, courses, and fellowships.

IARC determines if any chemical substance studied causes cancer.

In 1997 IARC classified *crystalline* silica as a Group 1, human carcinogen; their highest risk rating. The IARC Working Group of scientists concluded that overall the epidemiological findings supported increased lung cancer risks from inhaled *crystalline silica* (quartz and cristobalite) resulting from occupational exposure. *Amorphous (non crystalline)* silicas however, "have been studied less than crystalline silicas. They are generally less toxic than crystalline silica and are cleared more rapidly from the lung. There is *inadequate evidence* in humans and experimental animals for the carcinogenicity of *uncalcined* Diatomaceous Earth. Amorphous silica *is not classifiable as to its carcinogenicity to humans (Group 3)."*
http://monographs.iarc.fr/ENG/Monographs/vol68/volume68.pdf

OSHA (The US Occupational Safety And Health Administration): *Elimination of Silicosis Conference:* In 1997 based on the IARC's findings (above), in order to reduce workplace hazards, OSHA's Hazard Communication Standard (HCS) requires that products and materials containing 0.1 percent or more of crystalline silica to be labeled with a potential carcinogenic warning. OSHA significantly reduced the Permissible Exposure Limit (PEL) for crystalline silica. The current PEL for crystalline silica (quartz) in any product is restricted to less than 0.1 percent ($^1/_{10th}$ of 1 percent). Workers using crystalline silica products cannot be exposed to more than 0.1mg/m3 of crystalline silica in 8 hours. This is a very small amount of material. Websites: http://www.osha.gov http://www.crminerals.com/pages/silica_reulations.php

Poisons Centers (PCs): An extension of the WHO which provides toxicological information, medical treatment and analytical support for the management of toxic exposure cases, generally on a 24-hour-basis. Website: http://www.intox.org/

SORDSA: *Crystalline Silica: Health Hazards and Precautions:* February 1999.

http://www.asosh.org/Programmes/SORDSA/Crystalline_silica.htm

The Attorney General New York State Environmental Protection Bureau (EPA): *The Secret Hazards Of Pesticides—Inert Ingredients:* The Attorney General, Andrew M. Cuomo released an eye opening public warning on toxic chemical pesticides including *inert ingredients*. (February 1996).

www.oag.state.ny.us/environment/home_pesticides.html
www.oag.state.ny.us/press/reports/inerts/table_of_contents.html
www.oag.state.ny.us/press/reports/inerts/pesticide_report.pdf

United States Department Of Agriculture (USDA): *Evaluating DE Silicon Aerogel Dusts to Protect Stored Wheat from Insects,* Market Research Report #1038. (1975).

The World Health Organization: The WHO established in 1948 is headquartered in Geneva, Switzeralnd. It is a specialized agency of the United Nations that acts as a coordinating authority on international public health. The WHO estimates around 2 million poisonings each year worldwide. Pesticide exposure accounts for the greatest source being in agricultural chemical pest control. Chemicals may have immediate, acute effects, as well as chronic effects which result from long-term exposures. Chronic, low-level exposure to various chemicals may result in a number of adverse outcomes, including damage to the nervous and immune systems, impairment of reproductive function and development, cancer, and organ-specific damage. About 47,000 persons die every year as a result of such poisonings. Many of these, are unintentional (accidental), and can be prevented. The WHO recommends promoting the use of adequate safer pesticides, as well as decreasing the use of toxic chemicals.

www.who.int/entity/ifcs/documents/forums/forum1/en/FI-res2_en.pdf
http://www.who.int/water_sanitation_health/industrypollution/en/index2.html

Index

E

F

W

Dear Reader,

The author hopes you enjoy and benefit from reading and utilizing *Going Green Using Diatomaceous Earth How-To Tips.* Share it with your neighbors, family and friends to protect the health and safety of those you care about, and those around you. Not only that, enjoy your own better quality of life and live longer, free of disease. Health starts in the home with safer alternatives to toxic chemicals.

Your interest in this book is appreciated, and your encouragement is welcome. If you are interested in sharing your DE testimonials in future editions of this book or contacting the author for speaking engagements, book signings, book clubs or having a Skype video meeting with your club or group, or if you would like an article for a newspaper or your journal, or if you would like to retail this book on your website or with your business, feel free to contact the author.

Website: http://www.TuiRoseTips.com

OTHER BOOKS BY TUI ROSE

THE SMART, SIMPLE & SAFE SOLUTIONS GENIE SERIES

Coming soon

Green, Thrifty & Safer Home Solutions
1001 Easier, Faster, Healthier & More Resourceful Everyday Household Tips and Tricks,

www.outskirtspress/TuiRoseGreenHomeTips.com

Green, Thrifty & Safer Gardening Tips
501 Tips, Tonics & Tricks Plus Homemade Safer Pesticide Solutions

www.outskirtspress/TuiRoseGreenGardenTips.com

Cat Chat & Dog Pow Wow Pet Care Tips
101 Loving & Safe Tips For New Owners & New Pets

www.outskirtspress/TuiRosePetCareTips.com

Author's Home Website:
http://www.TuiRoseTips.com

/ergne, TN USA
`ebruary 2011

5832LV00001B/1/P